STUDENT BOOK • 2ND EDITION

iiTomo

いいとも2

Yoshie Burrows
Mami Izuishi
Yoko Nishimura-Parke
Rebecca Llewelyn

SERIES CONSULTANT

Professor Anthony J. Liddicoat

Pearson Australia
(a division of Pearson Australia Group Pty Ltd)
707 Collins Street, Melbourne, Victoria 3008
PO Box 23360, Melbourne, Victoria 8012
www.pearson.com.au
Copyright © Pearson Australia 2019 (a division of Pearson Australia Group Pty Ltd)
First published 2010 by Pearson Australia
2025 2024 2023 2022
10 9 8 7 6 5 4 3 2 1

Reproduction and communication for educational purposes
The Australian *Copyright Act* 1968 (the Act) allows a maximum of one chapter or 10% of the pages of this work, whichever is the greater, to be reproduced and/or communicated by any educational institution for its educational purposes provided that that educational institution (or the body that administers it) has given a remuneration notice to Copyright Agency Limited (CAL) under the Act. For details of the CAL licence for educational institutions contact Copyright Agency Limited (www.copyright.com.au).

Reproduction and communication for other purposes
Except as permitted under the Act (for example any fair dealing for the purposes of study, research, criticism or review), no part of this book may be reproduced, stored in a retrieval system, communicated or transmitted in any form or by any means without prior written permission. All enquiries should be made to the publisher at the address above.

This book is not to be treated as a blackline master; that is, any photocopying beyond fair dealing requires prior written permission.

Publisher: Sonia Davoine
Development Editor: Laura Wright
Content Developer: Chiharu Amano
Project Managers: Beth Zeme and Rekha Dureja
Production Editor: Laura Pietrobon
Lead Editor: Kylie Farmer
Editor: Masayuki Hirata
Illustrations: Tomomi Sarafov, Kai Lynk, Kae Sato-Goodsell, Boris Silvestri, Kanako and Yuzuru/Goodillustration.com
Rights and Permissions Editor: Amirah Fatin
Designer: Anne Donald
Typesetter: Leigh Ashforth
Proofreader: Miyuki Toi
Production Controller: Dominic Harman

Printed in Malaysia (CTP-PJB)

A catalogue record for this book is available from the National Library of Australia

ISBN: 9781488656729 (paperback)

Pearson Australia Group Pty Ltd ABN 40 004 245 943

Attributions
First Edition Series Consultant: Anthony J. Liddicoat
Second Edition Teaching Reviewers: Naoko Florence Abe and Rachel Francis

The following abbreviations are used in this list: t = top, b = bottom, l = left, r = right, c = centre.

Yoshie Burrows thanks Minami Ito for her greeting cards, Ayano Torisawa for donating her photos, and Catriona McKenzie for her professional guidance throughout.

Back cover: Getty Images: ferrantraite.
123RF: PaylessImages, p. 21br; Wang Tom, pp. 18 (frame 1), 25 (smiling girl), 61 (frame 3).
agefotostock: ankomando, p. 79 (poster).
Alamy Stock Photo: AF archive, pp. 75 (frame 3), 78b (frame 4); Archives du 7eme Art, pp. 73bl, 76 (frame 2, frame 4), 78b (frame 3); 78t (frame 2); Oote Boe 3, p. 18 (frame 4); Carlos Cardetas, p. 75 (frame 5), p. 78t (frame 3); CINEMA COLLECTION, p. 76 (frame 3); directphoto.bz, p. 40t; Jeremy Hoare, p. 36b; IE263, p. 20br; Japan Stock Photography, p. 4 (Japanese futon); Latham & Holmes, p. 2 (clock, frame 1); Richard Levine, p. 4 (kendo); Theodore Liasi, p. 79 (cosplay); MIXA, pp. 20tr, 21tl; okiphoto, p. 2 (clock, frame 3); Miguel Angel Muñoz Pellicer, p. 91l; Photo Japan, p. 37tr; Pictures Colour Library, pp. 90bl, 90br; PSL Images, p. 2 (clock, frame 2); Malcolm Schuyl, p. 37br; sozaijiten, p. 93; Studio Ghibli/Ronald Grant Archive, p. 78b (frame 2); Kirk Treakle, p. 21bl; United Archives GmbH, p. 75 (frame 2); VintageCorner, pp. 76 (frame 1), 78t (frame 1).
ASCII MEDIA WORKS – KADOKAWA: Kadokawa, p. 74 (book cover).
Davoine, Sonia: p. 74 (sign).
Dreamstime: Cardiae, p. 66 (bags); Dndavis, p. 66 (female student); Steven Frame, p. 66 (beach); Peter Mautsch/Maranso Gmbh, p. 66 (open book).
Flickr: Ken Lee, p. 79 (books).
Getty Images: Chel Beeson, p. 2 (clock, frame 4); Digital Vision, p. 27; Michael Krasowitz, p. 61 (frame 2); MIXA, pp. 43c, 43t; sot, p. 3br; stockstudioX, p. 4 (Japanese bath); ULTRA.F, p. 43b.
Goodrich, Alfie: pp. 3bl, 14, 15. 18 (frame 5).
Maeda, Masado: p. 8.
Morisawa Inc: The font software Uddkyo used in this product is provided by Morisawa Inc. UDDigiKyokasho is a trademark or registered trademarks of TypeBank Co, Ltd.
Newspix: Andrew Brownbill, p. 20tl.
Sedunary, Michael: p. 2bl.
Shutterstock: 300dpi, p. 66 (cinema); amenic181, p. 1bl; amnat11, p. 85bl; Apollofoto, p. 66 (female in blue); ArtSimulacra, p. 66 (handset); ATOMix, pp 73tr, 78b (frame 1), 78t (frame 4); Billion Photos, p. 66 (brushes); dach_chan, p. viii (left); DRogatnev, p. 51 (keys); enchanted_fairy, p. 77 (frame 3, frame 4); Faer Out, p. 37tl; Hannamariah, p. 4 (bed); Atsushi Hirao, p. 4 (Japanese breakfast); imtmphoto, p. 36t; kan_khampanya, p. 79 (kumamon merch); KPG_Mega, p. 85br; KPG_Payless, pp. 1t, 9b, 17bl, 17br, 17t, 18 (frame 3), 20bl, 36c; Kit Leong, p. 35br; LightField Studios, p. 57br; little_larc, p. 57bl; MeSamong, p. 77 (frame 2); MosayMay, p. 49tr; mTaira, pp. 1br, 57t; muzsy, p. 4 (soccer); octdesign, p. 61 (top mobile phone); Patrick Foto, p. 37bl; Igor Palamarchuk, p. 4 (eggs and avocadoes); Anurak Pongpatimet, p. 61 (frame 4); Kanisorn Pringthongfoo, p. 35tr; Denys Prykhodov, p. 61 (bottom mobile phone); Michael Shake, p. 58 (car); Ned Snowman, p. 49bl; spatuletail, p. 49br; Leon T, p. 66 (broom and dustpan); tulpahn, pp. 73br, 77 (frame 1); tumasia, p. 51 (car); VGstockstudio, pp. 61 (frame 1), 79 (girl); Vsevolodizotov, p. 66 (book stack); wizdata, pp. 18 (frame 2), 66 (male); walterericsy, p. 19; Windyboy, p. 79 (kumamon); John Wollwerth, p. 4 (Western bathroom); Lisa F. Young, p. viii (right); yukihipo, p. 85t; Vladimir Zhoga, p. 35bl; zkgwara, p. 75 (frame 4).

Disclaimer/s
The selection of Internet addresses (URLs) given in the iiTomo series were valid at the time of publication and chosen as being appropriate for use as a secondary education research tool. However, due to the dynamic nature of the internet, some addresses may have changed, may have ceased to exist since publication, or may inadvertently link to sites with content that could be considered offensive or inappropriate.

While the authors and publisher regret any inconvenience this may cause readers, no responsibility for any such changes or unforeseeable errors can be accepted by either the authors or the publisher.

The Publisher would like to thank the 30 teachers in Australia who donated their time to provide feedback and insight to contemporary teaching practices during the research phase for this new edition of iiTomo.

iiTomo Second Edition

Engaging and interactive Japanese language learning for Secondary Years

Clearly aligned to the Australian Curriculum, New South Wales Syllabus, Victorian Curriculum and Western Australian Curriculum, *iiTomo* 1–4 Second Edition offers new components and updated features for a motivating and supportive set of Japanese resources for students and teachers.

Student Book

A clear layout with improved, scaffolded content and visuals for Years 7–10 that focus on support and engagement and allow flexibility of use.

Reader+

Reader+ gives you access to the eBook version of your Student Book as well as multimedia content including audio, new grammar animations, new stroke order animations, new videos, interactive games and worksheets.

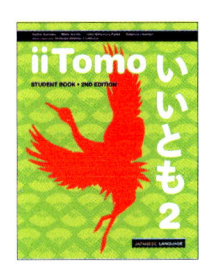

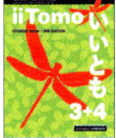

Activity Book

Updated engaging activities offer even more differentiated learning opportunities and reinforcement of key skills.

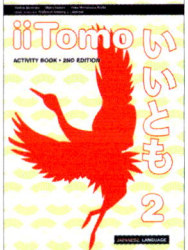

Teacher Guide

A comprehensive teacher support for beginning, relief and experienced teachers, making lesson preparation and implementation easier and saving you time. At a glance see all the resources linked to a chapter to make planning easier, selecting the right resources to suit your class or individuals. The Teacher Guide also includes clear learning goals, answers to the Student Book and Activity Book, audio scripts and teaching support notes.

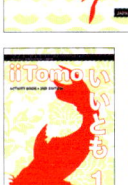

Teacher Reader+ and Audio Download

Access to all of the Student Reader+ content as well as a wealth of teacher materials including tests and associated audio, answers to all tests and worksheets, audio scripts, all of the Activity Book pages with answers ready for projection, weblinks and curriculum grids. Audio downloads are also available for ease of access.

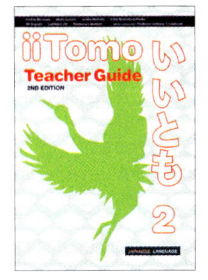

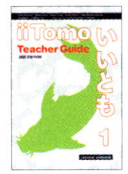

Also available: *iiTomo Senior* Student Book and Reader+ for Years 11 and 12.

Contents

How to use *iiTomo* vi
Japanese classroom expressions viii

	Chapter だい一か **1**	だい二か **17**	だい三か **35**	*Katakana* Chapter **49**
Title	いそがしいですか	学校、がんばろう！	学校のたのしいイベント	カタカナ
Content	Telling the time Daily routines Past events Lunch/extra activities	School year levels Subjects and timetable School life Self-introductions	Calendar months and dates Seasons School events and excursions, transport	Clothes Sport
Communicating	Ask and tell the time Talk about your daily routine Discuss what you do each day Describe what you eat for lunch	Say what year level you are in Talk about your school timetable Discuss the subjects you like and dislike	Talk about seasons, months and dates Discuss an event that you have planned on a certain date Talk about how you go to places Express how you get from one place to another	Read and write names in *katakana* Ask and say whether you can play a particular sport or not Talk about the clothes you often wear Describe what someone is wearing Talk about your favourite sport and music
Understanding	Making the past tense of verbs Using the particle と to connect nouns Using the particle に with time expressions	How to use negative form after the noun and negative form of な-adjectives The use of particles から 'from' and まで 'until'	Read and write dates of the month Using the particle で with transport The use of から and まで when talking about places Using the particle や when listing many things Using the particle よ at the end of the sentence	Read and write the 46 basic *katakana* Investigate the Japanese sound system with *katakana* Read and write some popular names in *katakana* Learn different ways to say 'to wear'
Particles	と に	から まで	に で から まで や よ	
Katakana* & *Kanji	時 学 校 半 分	先 生 中 高 年	見 行 食	46 basic katakana
Intercultural and cultural	Discover typical daily routine for students in Japan Find out what Japanese students eat for lunch Learn about club activities offered at schools in Japan Reflect on your own daily life in comparison to what you have learnt about Japan	Reflect on how school life in Japan is different from where you live Learn more about the Japanese school system Investigate subjects studied by students in Japan	Find out about and reflect on Japanese school events Understand the Japanese school calendar and compare it with your own Compare transport that students use in Japan with your own Learn about *ninjas*	Learn more about the Japanese writing system
Text types	Photo captions Clocks Pie chart Menu Speech Manga	Photo captions Timetable Online chat Self-introduction Manga	Photo captions Calendar Map Poster Profile	Photo captions
Putting it all together	Write a speech about your daily routine Create a video story of your daily routine Class survey on daily routines	Write an introductory blog post	Create a calendar of school events Design a webpage for a school excursion	

Chapter	だい四か 57	だい五か 73	だい六か 85
Title	しゅみは何ですか	どんなキャラクターですか	おまつりとおいわい
Content	Hobbies and sports Holidays Mobile phones	Parts of body describing physical appearance Anime and manga Using *katakana*	Birthdays and special occasions Festivals Receiving gifts
Communicating	Talk about hobbies Discuss where and how often you do various activities Talk about activities you did and did not do Write a diary entry in Japanese	Talk about people's physical appearance Talk about personality and abilities Talk about your favourite *anime* and manga characters	Say happy birthday Explain how you celebrate your birthday Talk about what you received on your birthday Discuss what you did on a special occasion
Understanding	Learn frequency words to use when talking about how often you do something Learn how to use the verb ending 〜ません でした. Use the particle で after a place word The use of particle に with some verbs Investigate how to call each other within a family	Using the て-form of い-adjectives and な-adjectives Build up a passage using conjunctions effectively	Particles に、から、を Say 'do it together' Using the verb もらいます 'to receive' Using particles から/に、を when constructing sentences about receiving presents Using particle で with みんな to mean 'all together'
Particles	で に		に から を
Kanji	買 休 山 川	目 口 耳 手	
Intercultural and cultural	Evaluate the place of homework during the summer break in Japan Analyse effects in the use of different scripts when referring to the same item	Explore how *anime* and *manga* are used in Japanese society Recognise Akihabara as a popular destination for *anime* and *manga* fans	Compare how people celebrate their birthdays and festivals in Japan and in Australia Learn about important birthdays in Japan Understand historical meanings of festivals Discover what you can find and buy in Japanese festivals
Text types	Photo captions Poster Picture diary Manga	Photo captions Manga	Photo captions Photo story Manga
Putting it all together	Create a survey about how teenagers spend their free time Write a picture diary about your best holiday	Create a hero or heroine Create a promotional video of yourself to send to a Japanese film company	Write a speech about birthdays in Australia Create a digital advertisement of a local festival

References 97

References 97
Counting 97
Adjectives 98
Verbs 98
Particles 100
Grammar summary 102

Vocabulary 106

Japanese – English 106
English – Japanese 111

How to use *iiTomo*

Let's explore what's in your *iiTomo Second Edition* Student Book, Reader+ and Activity Book.

Classroom expressions

You can find some useful classroom expressions that your teacher will be using and some you can learn to say on page viii to build on what you learnt in *iiTomo 1*. Have a go at practising these and using them during your Japanese lessons!

Katakana chapter

In this second edition, you learnt *hiragana* at the start of *iiTomo 1* and were exposed to some *katakana* throughout the chapters. You will find all *katakana* learning in *iiTomo 2* between chapter 3 and chapter 4.

The *katakana* chapter is designed for you to learn all 46 *katakana* (*dakuon/ handakuon*). Each page introduces 1–3 lines of *katakana*. The structure of these pages is the same:

- *Katakana* cards show how each character is written (stroke order) and are accompanied with modeling animations in your Reader+ eBook.
- *Let's read* provides reading practice focusing on carefully selected clothing and sports words.
- *Katakana in action* allows you to use the characters you are learning in context. The language introduced in this section gives you an opportunity to communicate in Japanese using the characters you have learnt. The Student Book will cover grammar points more thoroughly as you progress throughout the chapters; grammar is not the focus of the *katakana* chapter.

The other sections of this chapter are as per any other chapter and include Got it!, Vocabulary and Putting it all together. The corresponding Activity Book chapter provides opportunities for you to practise your *katakana* further.

You may cover the whole *katakana* chapter when you get to it, or at the start of the year, or even go through some pages at a time, then move on to another and back to the *hiragana* chapter.

Here are some features that are common to all chapters in your Student Book.

Chapter opener page

The first page of every chapter offers 3 **Let's get started** inquiry questions for you to consider as a group. The first question is factual, the second conceptual and the last debatable. They allow you to tap into your general knowledge and personal experience. Then, take the time to discuss the authentic visuals on the page in class to predict what you will be learning about, and do the related intercultural tasks in your Activity Book chapter opener which provides some cultural insight too. In your Reader+ eBook, there is a video you may want to watch now and revisit later on or you could wait until you get into the chapter to watch it.

The learning goals for each unit include:

- **Communicating** outlines the new communication skills you will be learning
- **Understanding** lists the different language items you will be covering, including new *kanji*
- **Intercultural and cultural** shows some of the cultural information you will explore and comparisons you will make to help develop your intercultural understanding.

My *katakana* and My *kanji*

These pages present *katakana* and *kanji* learning for the chapter with support for learning stroke order and pronunciation to help you read and write *katakana* and *kanji* quickly and confidently.

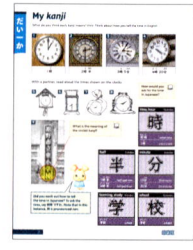

In your Reader+, stroke order animations will support you with your script writing skills and you copy or print out the character writing sheet for this purpose. The Activity Book includes some extra activities to help you practise your writing too.

Talk time

On these pages, you will get the opportunity to listen to and speak Japanese. Use the audio to rehearse your pronunciation and practise the speaking drills with a partner or in the class group. The English meaning for all new vocabulary is provided. Key sentences structures and grammar points are presented in red boxes with references to the relevant Got it! page.

Check it out!

On these pages, you will be able to read a variety of text types in Japanese. From brochures to personal presentations, to emails and websites, put your Japanese reading skills into practice and answer the comprehension prompts on the page.

Go for it!

Use your speaking skills to practise everything you have learnt so far. Practise with the given conversation first, and then have a go at creating your own, replacing the words in burgundy colour.

Got it?

Refer to these pages to develop your understanding of how the Japanese language works. The key language seen in that chapter is explained and supported by examples. For each chapter, your Reader+ offers a few animations that present the main language points in a visual way. You could watch these in class and/or in your own time.

At the back of your book, references pages provide a summary of the main language content. The **verb tables** are a great reference when you are unsure how to use the different verb forms in Japanese.

Power up!

Power up your Japanese learning with this section which gives you additional information about a more advanced language point related to the chapter.

Find out more!

These pages are where you will see everything you have learnt in the chapter come together in a Manga or another text type. Put your listening, speaking, reading and writing skills into practice while continuing to enhance your intercultural skills.

Vocabulary

At the end of each chapter is a summary of the new key language introduced in that chapter. Your Reader+ includes a more complete chapter vocabulary list. You can also look up words in the end of book Japanese—English and English—Japanese vocabulary lists.

Putting it all together!

The last page of each chapter includes some activities to choose from. You will work independently or collaboratively to put into practise the language and skills you have learnt, using technology when needed. You may even start working on an activity before you finish the chapter.

Icons used in *iiTomo* Student Book

- Listen to Japanese native speakers and practise your comprehension and pronunciation skills.
- Watch video content to support you when learning grammar patterns and stroke order or view a dialogue related to the content of the chapter.
- Develop your intercultural language learning awareness. Observe, notice, explore, compare and record your point of view.
- Work out Japanese language using deductive and thinking skills.
- Learn something extra about Japanese culture or language!
- Develop your 21st century skills through activities that involve collaboration, communication, critical thinking, creativity and ICT skills.

You will find handy reference charts inside the back cover of this book.

The *iiTomo 2* student components are:

- *iiTomo 2* Reader+ eBook
- *iiTomo 2* Student Book
- *iiTomo 2* Activity Book

We hope you will find your *iiTomo* resources clear and supportive and that they will give you an enjoyable, relevant and rewarding learning experience.

日本語のきょうしつのことば 🎧

Learn these classroom expressions to build on the ones you learnt in *iiTomo 1* and start using them as much as possible in class.

先生

Today's activities are (__).	きょうの かつどうは (__) です。
Let's revise (__).	(__) の ふくしゅうを しましょう。
Please start.	はじめて ください。
Please stop.	やめて ください。
Please speak louder.	大きい こえで いって ください。
Please say it slowly.	ゆっくり いって ください。
Please read page (__).	(__) ページを よんで ください。 (pe e ji)
Please read from the line (__).	(__) から よんで ください。
Please repeat after me.	あとに ついて いって ください。
Please put your hand up.	てを あげて ください。
Please write in (__).	(__) に かいて ください。
What do you think?	どう おもいますか。
What is the answer?	こたえは なん ですか。
Do you have any questions?	しつもんが ありますか。
Please answer the questions.	しつもんに こたえて ください。
Please discuss with your partner.	パートナーと はなして ください。 (pa a to na a)
Please do not speak.	はなさないで ください。
All together.	いっしょに。

中学生

Excuse me. / I am sorry.	すみません。
Can you please help me for a minute?	ちょっと いいですか。/ ちょっと すみません。
What page is it?	なん ページ ですか。 (pe e ji)
What is the meaning of (__)?	(__) の いみは なん ですか。
How do you say (__) in Japanese?	(__) は にほんごで なんと いいますか。
How do you read this *kanji*?	この かんじは どう よみますか。
How do you write?	どうやって かきますか。
Whose (__) is this?	これは だれの ですか。
It's mine. / It's (__)'s.	わたしの です。/ (__) さん / くんの です。
I forgot my homework.	しゅくだいを わすれました。
When is the test on (__)?	(__) の テストは いつ ですか。 (te su to)

desk	つくえ
chair	いす
Genkō yōshi	げんこうようし
worksheet	ワークシート (wa a ku shi i to)
marker	マーカー (ma a ka a)
app	アプリ (a pu ri)
projector	プロジェクター (pu ro je ku ta a)
locker	ロッカー (ro k ka a)

だい一か

いそがしいですか

1

LET'S GET STARTED! 🎥

- What is your typical daily routine like?
- What do extra-curricular activities mean to you?
- To what extent do extra-curricular activities help people?

1 6時に おきます。

2 おべんとうを たべます。

3 やきゅうを します。

Communicating

- Ask and tell the time
- Talk about your daily routine
- Discuss what you do each day
- Describe what you eat for lunch

Understanding

- Read and write five *kanji*: 時, 半, 分, 学, 校
- Use the particles に and と
- Create the past tense of verbs

Intercultural and cultural

- Discover typical daily routine for students in Japan
- Find out what Japanese students eat for lunch
- Learn about club activities offered at schools in Japan
- Reflect on your own daily life in comparison to what you have learnt about Japan

Before you start this chapter, go to page 1 of your Activity Book.

My kanji

What do you think each *kanji* means? Hint: Think about how you tell the time in English.

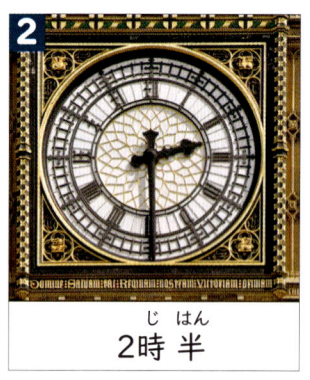

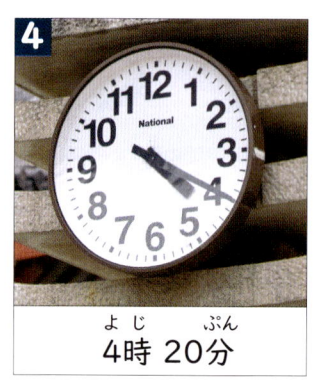

1. じ
   1時

2. じ　はん
   2時 半

3. じ　　ふん
   3時 5分

4. よじ　　ぷん
   4時 20分

With a partner, read aloud the times shown on the clocks.

5.
6.
7.
8.

9.

How would you ask for the time in Japanese?

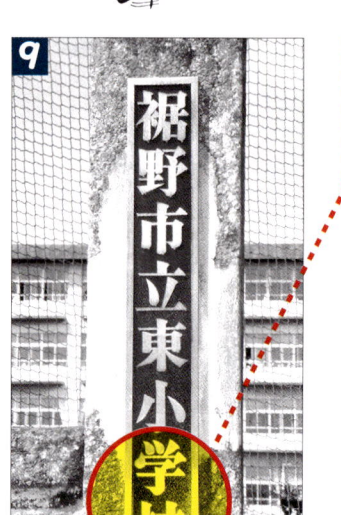

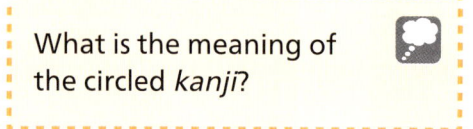

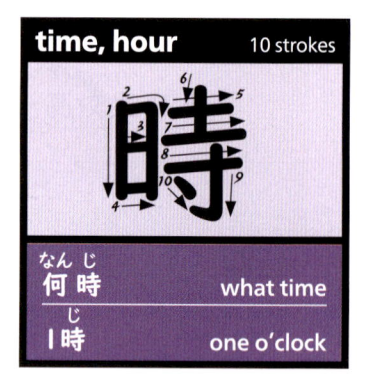

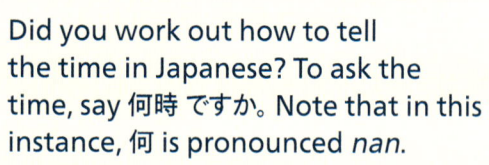

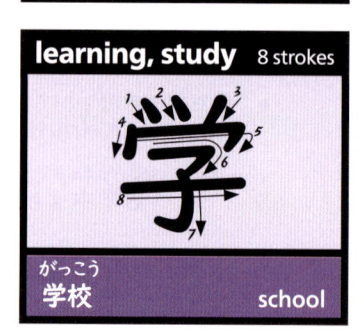

What is the meaning of the circled *kanji*?

time, hour	10 strokes
時	
なんじ 何時	what time
じ 1時	one o'clock

half	5 strokes
半	
じ はん 1時 半	half past one
よじ はん 4時 半	half past four

minute	4 strokes
分	
ふん 15分	15 minutes
ぷん 20分	20 minutes

learning, study	8 strokes
学	
がっこう 学校	school

school	10 strokes
校	
がっこう 学校	school

Did you work out how to tell the time in Japanese? To ask the time, say 何時 ですか。Note that in this instance, 何 is pronounced *nan*.

Talk time

Beat the clock! 🎧

With a partner, read the times aloud. Try to say them as quickly and as accurately as you can. When you are ready, your partner will set the clock! Compare your results.

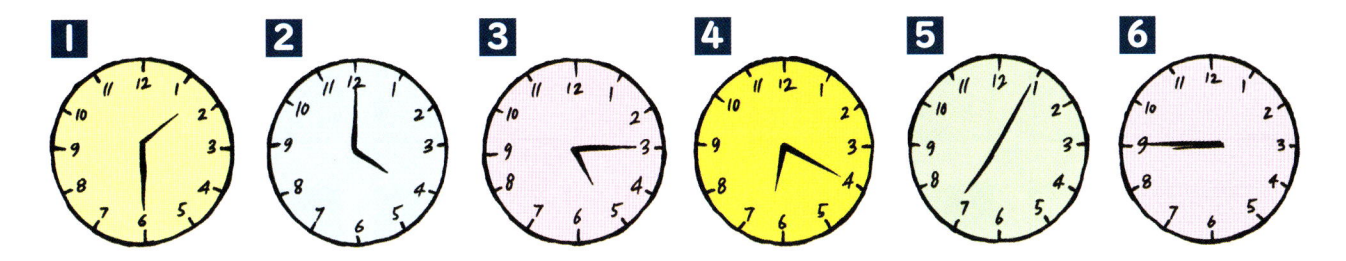

1. 2. 3. 4. 5. 6.

··

いま、何時ですか 🎧

With a partner, practise the conversations on this page. Using the prompts, give a different answer each time. Remember to swap roles.

1

すみません。いま、何時 ですか。

ああ。いま、3時半 です。

ありがとう ございます。

1.00　7.30　4.30
3.10　5.20　9.05

- What differences do you notice between these two conversations?
- What do they show about the relationships between the people?

2

ねえ。いま、何時？

いま？3時半。

ありがとう。

2.00　4.30　6.30
1.10　3.20　9.15

いま	now
何時	what time?
ああ	oh
ねえ	hey
すみません	excuse me

だい一か

3

Talk time
まい日 しますか 🎧

Let's look at ways we can talk about what we do every day. Listen to these dialogues to make meaning, and then practise with a partner.

1
A　まい日 はやく おきますか。
B　はい、はやく おきます。
　　いいえ、はやく おきません。

2
A　まい日 あさごはんを たべますか。
B　はい、たべます。
　　いいえ、たべません。

3
A　まい日 おふろに はいりますか。
B　はい、はいります。
　　いいえ、はいりません。
　　シャワーを あびます。
　　(sha wa a)

4
A　まい日 ぶかつを しますか。
B　はい、します。
　　いいえ、しません。

まい日	every day
はやく	early
おきます	wake up; get up
あさごはん	breakfast
たべます	eat
（お）ふろ	bath
はいります	get in; enter
シャワー (sha wa a)	shower
あびます	have/take (a shower)
ぶかつ	club activities

おふろに はいります。　p.13

- In Japan, you will find traditional Japanese sports, clothes, food, etc., and things that have been introduced more recently from other countries. Why do you think this is so?
- What do you think are the advantages or disadvantages of each?

中村久美さんの一日

Listen to this conversation, and then practise it with a partner. As you get more confident, answer using the times that you would normally do things.

1
中村 久美さんは 何時に おきますか。

そう ですね。
7時15分に おきます。

2
何時に 学校に いきますか。

ええと、8時10分に 学校に いきます。

3
何時に うちに かえりますか。

ええと、7時に うちに かえります。

4
じゃ、何時に ねますか。

そう ですね。
11時に ねます。

うち	home
かえります	go home; return
ねます	sleep
じゃ	well then

[Person]は [time]に [activity]を [verb]。
[Person]は [time]に [place]に いきます。

p.13

だいーか

Check it out!

Japanese students' daily routines

One hundred students from a school in 九州 (きゅうしゅう) answered an アンケート (a n ke e to) (questionnaire). Find out about their daily routines.

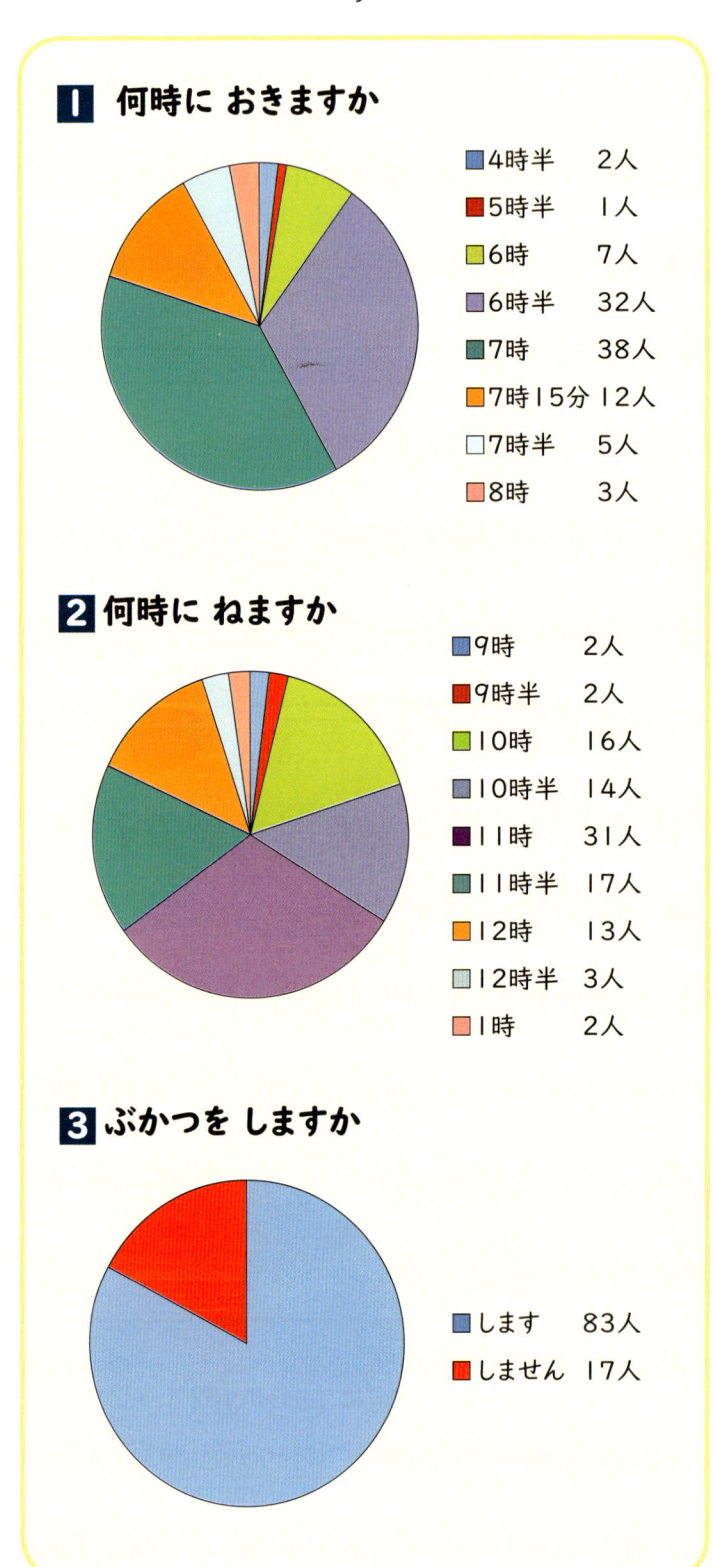

1 何時に おきますか

- 4時半　　2人
- 5時半　　1人
- 6時　　　7人
- 6時半　　32人
- 7時　　　38人
- 7時15分　12人
- 7時半　　5人
- 8時　　　3人

2 何時に ねますか

- 9時　　　2人
- 9時半　　2人
- 10時　　 16人
- 10時半　 14人
- 11時　　 31人
- 11時半　 17人
- 12時　　 13人
- 12時半　 3人
- 1時　　　2人

3 ぶかつを しますか

- します　　83人
- しません　17人

Comprehension questions

Interpret the survey results and discuss your findings in small groups.

1. What time do most students get up?
2. What time do most students go to bed?
3. What did you notice about the students' participation in ぶかつ?
4. Survey your class about their routines and show your findings in a pie chart. Compare the results.

- Consider daily routines and school programs. What differences do you notice between Japanese and Australian students?
- Why do you think these differences exist?
- Do you think that all students in Japan would have routines that are similar to those of the students surveyed?

Talk time
鈴木たかしくんの土よう日 🎧

To talk about past events, you need to know the past tense of verbs.

With a partner and using the dialogue below as an example, practise talking about what 鈴木(すずき)くん did last Saturday. Remember to change **ます** ending to **ました** to make past tense of verb.

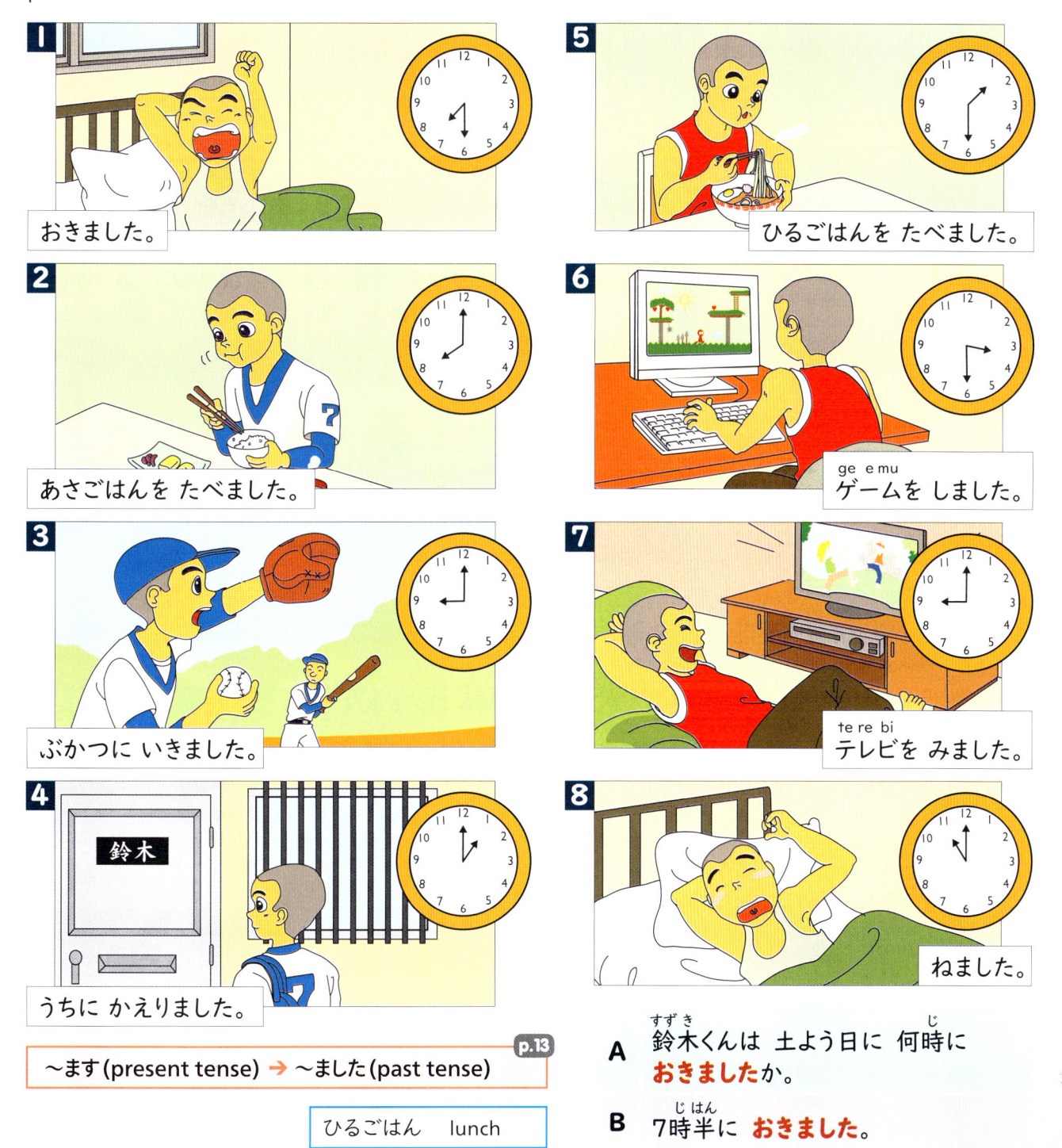

1 おきました。

2 あさごはんを たべました。

3 ぶかつに いきました。

4 うちに かえりました。

5 ひるごはんを たべました。

6 ゲーム(ge e mu)を しました。

7 テレビ(te re bi)を みました。

8 ねました。

〜ます (present tense) → 〜ました (past tense)　p.13

ひるごはん　lunch

A 鈴木(すずき)くんは 土よう日に 何時(じ)に **おきました**か。

B 7時(じ)半(はん)に **おきました**。

だい一か

Talk time
ひるごはんに何をたべますか 🎧

What do you eat for lunch? Let's look at the menu at 中村(なかむら)さんの 学校.

7月の きゅうしょく

16日	17日	18日	19日	20日
月よう日	火よう日	水よう日	木よう日	金よう日
ごはん	ライス (ra i su)	トースト (tō su to)	みそ ラーメン (ra a me n)	サフラン ライス (sa fu ra n ra i su)
さかな じゃがいも つけもの ぎゅうにゅう	コロッケ (ko ro k ke) スープ (su u pu) つけもの ぎゅうにゅう	チリコンカン (chi ri ko n ka n) サラダ (sa ra da) くだもの ぎゅうにゅう	はるまき くだもの ぎゅうにゅう	ハンバーグ (ha n ba a gu) じゃがいも スープ (su u pu) ぎゅうにゅう

With a partner, practise the dialogue. Then, swap roles.

A ひるごはんに 何を たべますか。
B ひるごはんに きゅうしょくを たべます。
そして、ぎゅうにゅうを のみます。

ひるごはん	lunch
きゅうしょく	school lunch
じゃがいも	potato
ぎゅうにゅう	milk
のみます	drink

- What are the benefits of きゅうしょく? 🔗
- If you had きゅうしょく at your school, what would you like on the menu? How would it differ from a typical menu in Japan?

[Meal]に [food item]を たべます。　p.13
[Drink/Soup]を のみます。

八　　8

おべんとう 🎧

Practise conversing with a partner using the model dialogue below.

1 おべんとう

2 おべんとう

3 おちゃ

A　ひるごはんに 何を たべますか。
B　ひるごはんに おべんとうを たべます。
　　そして、おちゃを のみます。

A　だれと おべんとうを たべますか。
B　ともだちと おべんとうを たべます。

Look closely at the おべんとう. What differences do you notice between Japanese おべんとう and the lunches you take to school?

[Person] と [activity] を [verb]。　p.13

- What do you notice in this photograph?
- Discuss how you would feel about eating your lunch in your homeroom every day.

ともだちと おべんとうを たべます。

(お)べんとう	packed lunch
(お)ちゃ	tea
だれ	who
だれと	with whom?

だい一か

Check it out!
鈴木くんのスピーチ

suzuki
鈴木くん's class is going to have a teleconference with their pen-pal class in Japan. He was asked to prepare a speech to present.

1
みなさん、こんにちは。
ぼくは 鈴木(すずき) たかし です。

2
ぼくは まい日 7時(じ)に おきます。
そして、あさごはんを たべます。
8時(じ)に 学校(がっこう)に いきます。
ひるごはんに おべんとうを たべます。
ともだちと たべます。

3
4時半(じはん)に ぶかつを します。
ぼくは やきゅうぶの メンバー(me n ba a) です。
やきゅうが 大好き です。
まい日 ぶかつを します。
土よう日も ぶかつを します。

4
まい日 7時(じ)に うちに かえります。
それから、ばんごはんを たべます。
9時(じ)に テレビ(te re bi)を みます。
そして、11時(じ)に ねます。

5
では、これで おわります。
ありがとう ございました。

〜ぶ	(activity) club
メンバー (me n ba a)	member
ばんごはん	dinner

Here are some tips to help you write your own Japanese speech. To begin, always greet the audience (for example, みなさん、こんにちは). End your speech by saying, では、これで おわります。(Well then, this is the end of my speech.). Do not forget to say thank you – ありがとう ございました!

Go for it!
インタビュー

Your class is working on a survey about daily routine. Practice this conversation with a partner.

Person A
すみません。 インタビュー いい ですか。

Person B
はい どうぞ。

Person A
まい日　　　何時に おきますか。

Person B
ええと、　　6時50分に　　　　おきます。
　　　　　　7時15分に

Person A
じゃあ、　　まい日　　　あさごはんを たべますか。

Person B
はい、 たべます。

いいえ、 たべません。

Person A
まい日　　　ぶかつを しますか。

Person B
はい、 まい日 ぶかつを します。　　そして、　　火よう日に　　スポーツを します。
いいえ、 しません。　　　　　　　　でも、　　　水よう日に

Person A
何時に　　　うちに かえりますか。

Person B
4時半に

5時10分に　　うちに かえります。

6時15分に

Person A
はやく ねますか。

Person B
　　　　　　　　　　　　　　　　　9時半に
はい、　　はやく ねます。　　まい日　10時に　　ねます。
いいえ、　はやく ねません。　　　　　12時に

Person A
どうも ありがとう ございました。

Telling the time on the hour and at half past

1時	いちじ	7時	**しち**じ	1時半	いちじはん
2時	にじ	8時	はちじ	2時半	にじはん
3時	さんじ	9時	**く**じ	3時半	さんじはん
4時	**よ**じ	10時	じゅうじ	4時半	**よ**じはん
5時	ごじ	11時	じゅういちじ	5時半	ごじはん
6時	ろくじ	12時	じゅうにじ	6時半	ろくじはん

Telling the minutes

5分	ごふん
10分	じゅっぷん
15分	じゅうごふん
20分	にじゅっぷん
25分	にじゅうごふん
30分	さんじゅっぷん
35分	さんじゅうごふん
40分	よんじゅっぷん
45分	よんじゅうごふん
50分 or 10分まえ	ごじゅっぷん or じゅっぷん まえ
55分	ごじゅうごふん

Power up!
More minutes

1分	いっぷん	6分	ろっぷん	
2分	にふん	7分	ななふん	
3分	さんぷん	8分	はちふん	はっぷん
4分	よんぷん	9分	きゅうふん	
5分	ごふん	10分	じゅっぷん	

Asking and telling the time

いま、何時 ですか。	What time is it now?
いま、3時半 です。	It is now 3.30.
いま、3時15分 です。	It is now 3.15.

Daily routines

まい日 [activity]を [verb]か。	Do you do [activity] every day?
まい日 ぶかつを しますか。	Do you do club activities every day?
はい、まい日 ぶかつ を します。	Yes, I do club activities every day.
いいえ、しません。	No, I do not.

Past events

Making past tense for verbs is easy. Change the verb ending ます to ました.

Present tense: 〜ます		Past tense: 〜ました	
おきます	get up; wake up	おきました	got up; woke up
いきます	go	いきました	went
たべます	eat	たべました	ate

何時に おき**ました**か。   What time did you get up?

土よう日に 何時に ね**ました**か。   On Saturday, what time did you go to bed?

7時15分に 学校に いき**ました**。   I went to school at 7.15.

The particle と

You have learnt that the particle と means 'and', and it is used to connect nouns.

にく**と** やさいを たべます。   I eat meat **and** vegetables.

The particle と can also be used to mean 'with' someone.

ともだち**と** きゅうしょくを たべます。   I eat school lunch **with** friends.

The particle に

The particle に is used with various time expressions, such as year, month, day and time, to indicate a specific point of time. It can be translated as 'at', 'on' or 'for'.

何時**に**   **at** what time   月よう日**に**   **on** Monday

7時**に**   **at** 7.00   あさごはん**に**   **for** breakfast

The particle に can also mean 'in'.

おふろ**に**   **in** the bath

What do you eat for lunch?

When talking about eating habits, you use に after the meal you are talking about; for example, 'for lunch' is ひるごはんに.

ひるごはん**に** 何を たべますか。   What do you eat **for** lunch?

ひるごはん**に** おべんとうを たべます。   I eat a packed lunch **for** lunch.

Find out more!
まい日 いそがしいです! 🎧

Year 8 students in Japan were asked to create photo journals to show Australian students their daily life in Japan. Here is one of them.

1. みなさん、こんにちは。
わたしは 本田(ほんだ) あやか です。

2. まい日 6時45分(じ ふん)に おきます。

3. そして、あさごはんを たべます。
それから、7時50分(じ ぷん)に 学校(がっこう)に いきます。

4. 12時(じ)に ともだちと おひるごはんを たべます。
ひるごはんに おべんとうを たべます。
そして、おちゃを のみます。 おべんとうは おいしい です。

5. 4時(じ)に ぶかつに いきます。
わたしは テニス(te ni su)ぶの メンバー(me n ba a) です。 わたしは テニス(te ni su)が 大好き です。 だから、まい日 ともだちと ぶかつを します。

十四
14

6 6時半に うちに かえります。

7 7時に 母と ばんごはんを たべます。

8 8時に しゅくだいを します。

9 そして、9時に テレビを みます。
わたしは テレビが 大好き です。
まんがも よみます。

10 10時半に おふろに はいります。

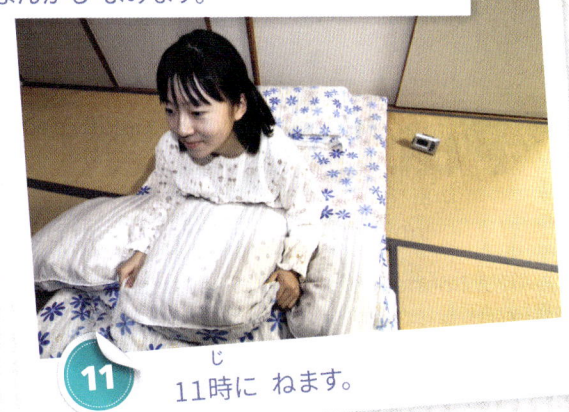

11 11時に ねます。

だい一か

Comprehension questions

1. List three leisure activities that あやか enjoys.
2. What time does あやか eat her lunch? What does she eat and drink?
3. Explain her extra-curricular activity.
4. How would you improve あやか's daily routine? Rewrite what she has written with your changes.

Consider あやか's daily routine. How do you think it is similar to or different from your own? To show the similarities and differences, create a Venn diagram in Japanese.

| しゅくだい | homework |

十五

My vocabulary

Essential たんご Practise reading this chapter's key たんご with a partner. As you read words aloud, cover the English and check that you know what each one means. Then, write them out to build your own list.

Asking and telling the time

すみません	excuse me
いま	now
何時 (なんじ)	what time
～時 (じ)	… o'clock

Talking about daily routine

まい日 (にち)	every day
はやく	early
あさごはん	breakfast
ひるごはん	lunch
ばんごはん	dinner
(お)ふろ	bath
学校 (がっこう)	school
ぶかつ	club activities (at school)
うち	home
きゅうしょく	school lunch
(お)べんとう	packed lunch
(お)ちゃ	green tea
しゅくだい	homework
だれ	who

Verbs

おきます	to wake up; get up	かえります	to go home; return
たべます	to eat	ねます	to sleep
はいります	to get in; enter	のみます	to drink
(シャワーを) あびます (shawaa)	to have/take (a shower)	おわります	to finish

Additional vocabulary

ああ	oh	ぎゅうにゅう	milk
ねえ	hey	コロッケ (korokke)	croquette(s)
じゃ	well then	トースト (tōsuto)	toast(s)
～ぶ	(activity) club	チリコンカン (chirikonkan)	chilli con carne
メンバー (menbaa)	member	みそ	soy bean paste
インタビュー (intabyuu)	interview	はるまき	spring roll(s)
いいですか。	Is it OK?	サフランライス (safuranraisu)	saffron rice
じゃがいも	potato(es)		

Putting it all together 🔑

Class survey

Conduct a class survey on daily routines (アンケート (ankeeto)). You need to ask at least five questions in Japanese:

- [ ] what time they get up and go to bed
- [ ] whether they eat breakfast or not
- [ ] what they eat for lunch
- [ ] what time they go home
- [ ] what time they have dinner.

My daily routine video

Create a video story of your daily routine and add a narration in Japanese.

My daily routine speech

Using the speech script of 鈴木くんのスピーチ (supiichi) on page 10 as a model, write a speech about your daily routine.

- [ ] Start your speech with a greeting,
- [ ] include information about your daily routine including:
    - time to get up and go to bed
    - breakfast, lunch and dinner
    - after school activities
- [ ] finish with a closing remark.

だい二か
学校、がんばろう！

2

LET'S GET STARTED! 🎥

- What is a typical school day for you?
- Look at the pictures. What do you think might be some similarities and differences between your school and schools in Japan?
- Do you think students should clean the school each day? Why? Why not?

1 こく語の 先生(せんせい)は きびしい です。

2 1時かんめは りか です。

3 おんがくが 好き ですか。

Communicating
- Say what year level you are in
- Talk about your school timetable
- Discuss the subjects you like and dislike

Understanding
- Read and write five *kanji*: 先, 生, 中, 高, 年
- How to use negative form after the noun and negative form of な-adjectives
- The use of particles から and まで

Intercultural and cultural
- Reflect on how school life in Japan is different from where you live
- Learn more about the Japanese school system
- Investigate subjects studied by students in Japan

Before you start this chapter, go to page 17 of your Activity Book.

17　　十七

My *kanji*
さちさんの学校

森(もり) さち is introducing her teacher and siblings.

1
森(もり) さち です。
中学生(ちゅうがくせい) です。

2
山口先生(やまぐち せんせい) です。すう学(がく)の 先生(せん せい) です。

3 あね
あねの かおり です。高校生(こうこうせい) です。

4 おとうと
おとうとの りく です。小学生(しょうがくせい) です。

5
小学校(しょうがっこう)

- You know 小 means 'small'. If 学校 means 'school', what might 小学校(しょうがっこう) and 小学生(しょうがくせい) mean?
- You have learnt 大 as 'big', what do you think 大学(だいがく) means?
- 中(ちゅう) means 'middle'. Does your school have a 中学校(ちゅうがっこう)?
- What do you think a 高校(こうこう) is?

十八

18

Here are five new *kanji* for you to practise, and three *kanji* you already learnt with another reading (red *kanji* cards).

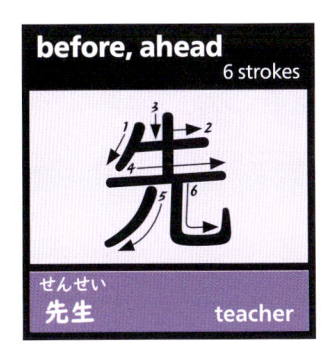

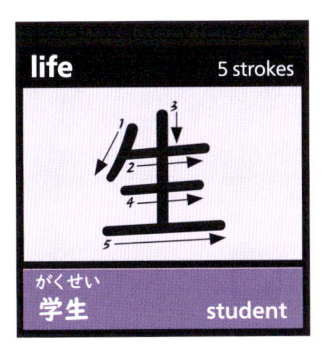

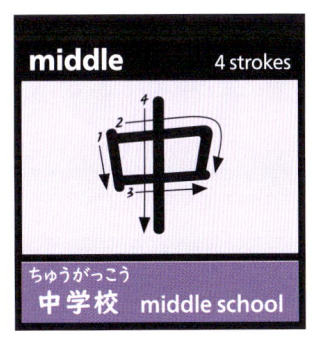

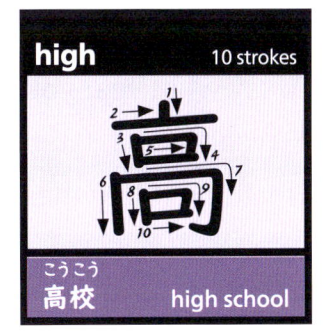

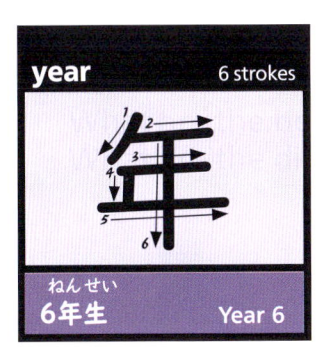

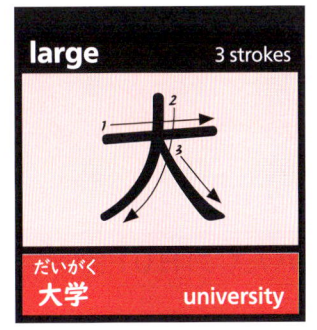

before, ahead (6 strokes)	life (5 strokes)	middle (4 strokes)	high (10 strokes)
先	生	中	高
せんせい 先生 teacher	がくせい 学生 student	ちゅうがっこう 中学校 middle school	こうこう 高校 high school

year (6 strokes)	small (3 strokes)	large (3 strokes)	learning, study (8 strokes)
年	小	大	学
ねんせい 6年生 Year 6	しょうがっこう 小学校 primary school	だいがく 大学 university	すう学 maths (がく)

しでんのうじ ちゅうがっこう
四天王寺 中学校

What sort of school is shown in this picture?

Review the comparative charts below. What differences do you notice between Australian school year levels and Japanese year levels?

Australian year level	Japanese school	Japanese year level
Year 7		中学 1年生
Year 8	ちゅうがっこう 中学校	中学 2年生
Year 9		中学 3年生
Year 10		高校 1年生
Year 11	こうこう 高校	高校 2年生
Year 12		高校 3年生

School	Student
小	しょうがくせい 小学生
中	ちゅうがくせい 中学生
高	こうこうせい 高校生

だい二か

19   十九

Talk time
何年生ですか 🎧

To say what year you are in at school, say the number of your year followed by 年 (ねん) (year) and 生 (せい) (student). Let's have a look at how students say what year they are in. Practise reading these sentences aloud.

1.
アリーシャ (a ri i sha) さんは 何年生 (なんねんせい) ですか。
わたしは 8年生 (ねんせい) です。

2.
大山 (おおやま) くんは 何年生 (なんねんせい) ですか。
ぼくは 中学 (ちゅうがく) 2年生 (ねんせい) です。

3.
川田 (かわだ) くんは 何 (なん) 年生 (ねんせい) ですか。
高校 (こうこう) 3年生 (ねんせい) です。

4.
鈴木 (すずき) さんは 何年生 (なんねんせい) ですか。
大学 (だいがく) 1年生 (ねんせい) です。

> When students talk among themselves, they often shorten the way they say the year they are in. For example, they might just say 中 (ちゅう) 2 or 高 (こう) 3.

> What differences do you notice between the Japanese students' answers and the answer given by the Australian student in photo 1?

何年生 (なんねんせい)　what grade

二十

何年生？

With a partner, practise the model conversation using the clues to ask what year someone is in.

A 山川くんは 何年生 ですか。
B 小学5年生 です。

Turn to page 30 for a complete list of the Australian and Japanese school years.

1 小学生

山川 なおと
小学5年生

山田 あい
小学4年生

2 中学生

林 ゆみ
中学1年生

本田 たかみ
中学2年生

3 高校生

西山 ももこ
高校1年生

上田 みく
高校1年生

だい二か

21

二十一

Talk time

学校のかもく 🎧

Practise talking about these school subjects with a partner.

A [Subject]が 好き ですか。
B はい、[subject]が 好き です。
いいえ、[subject]は 好き じゃない です。
[Subject]は あんまり...。

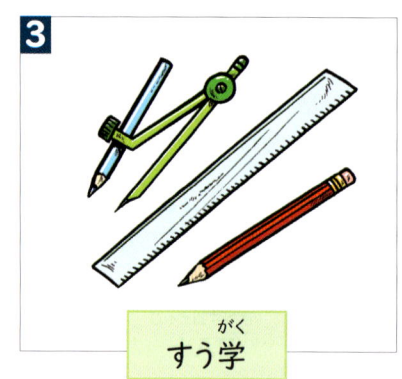

1 えい語

2 こく語

3 すう学

4 おんがく

5 りか

6 びじゅつ

7 たいいく

8 ぎじゅつ

9 れきし　ちり　しゃかい

10 かていか

Just as you study English, Japanese students study Japanese. This subject is called こく語, which means 'national language'.

| かもく | school subjects |

だい二か

ニ十ニ

22

1時かんめはおんがくですか

With a partner, discuss your school timetable and when you have which classes.

1. ひろしくん、1時かんめは何(なん)ですか。
1時かんめは すう学(がく) です。

2. てつやくん、1時かんめは えい語 ですか。
えい語？ えい語 じゃない です。1時かんめは こく語 です。

3. おんがくは 何時かんめ ですか。
おんがくは 4時(よ)かんめ です。

4. すみません。ひるやすみは 何時 から 何時 まで ですか。
ひるやすみは 12時半 から 1時半 まで です。

Remember 何 has two readings: なに and なん。何時かんめ is read なんじかんめ.

〜時かんめ	period —
何時かんめ	what period
〜じゃない です	it is not —
ひるやすみ	lunch break
から	from
まで	until

[Number]時かんめは [subject]です。
[Subject]じゃない です。

23　二十三

Check it out!
さえさんの時かんわり

What time does each lesson start? Practise asking and answering with a partner.

中学1年生の時かんわり

		月	火	水	木	金	土
1	9:00-9:50	すう学	こく語	たいいく	びじゅつ	すう学	こく語
2	10:00-10:50	こく語	えい語	たいいく	どうとく	りか	えい語
3	11:00-11:50	おんがく	かていか	しゃかい	こく語	えい語	すう学
4	12:00-12:50	しゃかい	かていか	えい語	すう学	しゃかい	りか
	12:50-1:35	→ ひるやすみ					
5	1:35-2:25	りか	しゃかい	こく語	えい語	たいいく	
6	2:35-3:25	えい語	たいいく	びじゅつ	すう学	こく語	
	3:25-3:45	そうじ					

Read さえ's email describing a day at school based on her timetable.
Then, choose another day and describe it in your notebook.

New Message
To:
Subject: 時かんわり

月よう日の 1時かんめは すう学 です。
2時かんめは こく語 です。4時かんめは しゃかい です。
ひるやすみは 12時50分 から 1時35分 まで です。
ひるごはんに おべんとうを たべます。ともだちと
はなします。5時かんめは りか です。りかは
むずかしい です。3時25分 から 3時45分 まで
そうじを します。 そうじは 好き じゃない です。

Compare your timetable with さえ's. Create a Venn diagram in Japanese to show the similarities and differences. Why do you think these similarities and differences exist?

Comprehension question

- What year level do you think さえ is in?

時かんわり	timetable
どうとく	ethics
そうじ	cleaning
むずかしい	difficult

Talk time
好きなかもく 🎧

This is my timetable. Every week I have lots of subjects to study. Some subjects I like more than others. Can you find them?

What would you say about your subjects? Share your opinions with a partner.

だい二か

月よう日の 1時かんめは すう学 です。すう学が 好き です。 たのしい です。

水よう日の 3時かんめは えい語 です。えい語は 一ばん 好きな かもく です。

中学2年生

	月	火	水	木	金	土
1	すう学	えい語	びじゅつ	しゃかい	すう学	えい語
2	こく語	すう学	びじゅつ	おんがく	こく語	すう学
3	りか	しゃかい	えい語	りか	どうとく	こく語
4	えい語	おんがく	しゃかい	えい語	えい語	りか

ひるやすみ

	月	火	水	木	金	土
5	たいいく	こく語	すう学	かていか	しゃかい	
6	たいいく	りか	こく語	かていか	すう学	

そうじ

木よう日の 5時かんめと 6時かんめは かていか です。かていかは 好き じゃない です。ちょっと つまらない です。

金よう日の 5時かんめは しゃかい です。しゃかいは にがてな かもく です。でも、好き です。

p.31

[Subject]が 好き です。
[Subject]は 好き じゃない です。
[Subject]は 一ばん 好きな かもく です。
[Subject]は にがてな かもく です。
一ばん むずかしい かもくは [subject] です。
一ばん おもしろい かもくは [subject] です。

一ばん 好きな かもく	most favourite subject
一ばん むずかしい かもく	most difficult subject
ちょっと	little bit
つまらない	boring
にがてな かもく	a subject that I am weak at

25

二十五

Check it out!

日本たのしい！フォーラム

Students from Australia and Japan are chatting in an online フォーラム (fō ra mu).

(^_^)/ ミックシー (mi k kushi i) です。 高校2年生 (こうこう ねんせい) です。 きょう、3時かんめは えい語 でした。 えい語は むずかしい ですね。

(=^_^=) そう ですね。 わたしも 2時かんめは えい語 でした。 えい語は にがてな かもく です。 でも、好き です。 ミックシー (mi k kushi i) さんは？

えい語は あんまり…。

ティムタム (ti muta mu) です。 (^_^)/ 10年生 (ねんせい) です。 えい語は 一ばん 好きな かもく です。 でも、 すう学 (がく) は とても むずかしい です。 だから、好き じゃない です。

ほんとう ですか。 すう学 (がく) は たのしい です。 大 (だい) 好き ですよ。 ぼくは ジェーベー (je e be e) です。 (^_^)/ 9年生 (ねんせい) です。

すう学 (がく)？ いやだ！ すう学 (がく) は つまらない ですよ。(z_z) でも、おんがくは とても たのしい です。 だから、一ばん好きな かもく です。

そう ですね！ わたしも おんがくが 大 (だい) 好き です！
o(^^o) (o^^o) (o^^)o

金よう日に 日本語の しけんが あります。
こわい！(;^_^) 日本語の しけんは 11時から 12時半 まで です。

いやだ！ でも、がんばって ください。

がんばってね！ (=^_^=)

- いやだ means 'yuck, terrible' and it is the casual form of いやです. Why do you think いやだ was used in this chat room?
- Why do you think they said がんばって? What would you say in a similar situation?

きょう	today
でした	was
ほんとう	true; really
いやだ	yuck; terrible
しけん	exam
がんばって ください。	Please do your best.

Comprehension question

- Which students do you think are from Japan? Which are from Australia? Why?

Create your own avatar and chat about your subjects with other students on your class or an online forum.

二十六

26

Go for it!

自己紹介 🎧

Listen to たくみ's 自己紹介 (じこしょうかい) (self-introduction) from his profile page. Then, record your own to tell たくみ all about you.

だい二か

自己紹介 (じこしょうかい)

Takumi Yamakawa

はじめまして。 山川(やまかわ) たくみ です。 日本人 です。 15さい です。

かぞくは 五人 です。 父と 母と あにが 二人と ぼく です。

大阪(おおさか)に すんで います。

ぼくは 中学2年生(ちゅうがくねんせい) です。 学校は 9時 から 4時 まで です。

一ばん 好きな かもくは すう学(がく) です。 とても おもしろい です。 でも、 りかは むずかしい です。 だから、 にがてな かもく です。

4時 から 4時半 まで 学校を そうじ します。 そうじは 好き じゃない です。

でも、 4時半 から 6時半 まで ぶかつを します。 ぶかつは たのしい です。

6時半に うちに かえります。

みなさん、 どうぞ よろしく おねがい します。

| どうぞ よろしく おねがい します。 | I am very pleased to meet you. |

27 ニ十七

Find out more!
アイザイアーのスクラップブック

Isaiah Taumera is on exchange in Japan for a year. He is keeping a スクラップ ブック (sukura p pu bu k ku) so he can share his experiences with his classmates when he returns home.

1. ぼくの せいふく です。 かっこいいな!

2. 月よう日 から 土よう日 まで 学校に いきます。

3. いりぐちで うわばきを はきます。

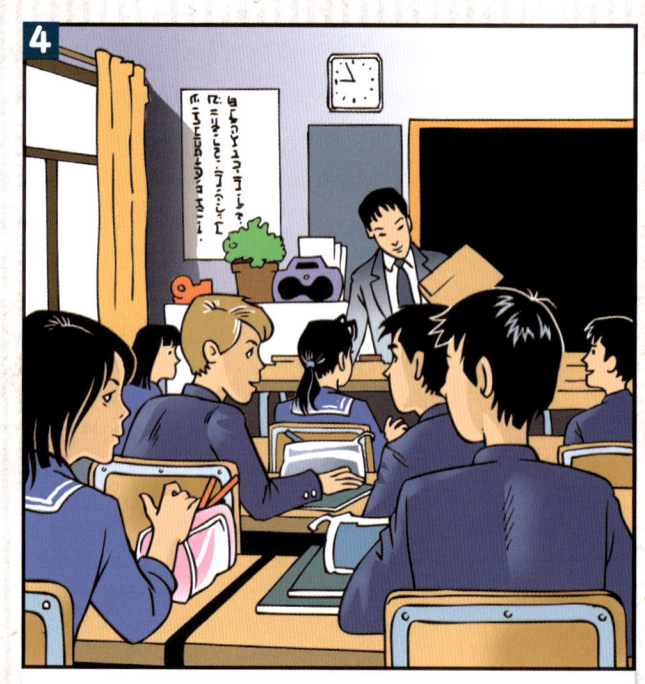

4. 岸田先生(きしだせんせい) です。 岸田先生(きしだせんせい)は やさしい です。

だい二か
二十八

だい二か

5. ぼくの ホームルーム です。ホームルームは えい語 とこく語と しゃかいと すう学の きょうしつ です。

6. ひるやすみは 12時半 から 1時20分 まで です。まい日 おべんとうを たべます。

7. 火よう日の 5時かんめは たいいく です。サッカーを します。

8. 火よう日の 6時かんめは りか です。りかは 好きな かもく です。

9. そして、きょうしつを そうじ します。それから、うちに かえります。

- What do you think might be important for Japanese students to know if they were to visit your school?
- What do you think might be unusual or different for them?
- In Japanese, create a scrapbook or photo journal of a day in your life at school. Try to include information that a Japanese exchange student visiting your school might find helpful.

Comprehension question

- With a partner, discuss some of the differences between Isaiah's day at school and your day. What are some of the similarities?

せいふく	uniform
いりぐちで	at the entrance
うわばきを はきます	put on indoor shoes
ホームルーム	homeroom
きょうしつ	classroom

Got it?

Australian and Japanese school years

Australia	Japan
Year 1	しょうがく1年生 (小学1年生)
Year 2	しょうがく2年生 (小学2年生)
Year 3	しょうがく3年生 (小学3年生)
Year 4	しょうがく4年生 (小学4年生)
Year 5	しょうがく5年生 (小学5年生)
Year 6	しょうがく6年生 (小学6年生)

Australia	Japan
Year 7	ちゅうがく1年生 (中学1年生)
Year 8	ちゅうがく2年生 (中学2年生)
Year 9	ちゅうがく3年生 (中学3年生)
Year 10	こうこう1年生 (高校1年生)
Year 11	こうこう2年生 (高校2年生)
Year 12	こうこう3年生 (高校3年生)

Australia	Japan
First year, university	だいがく1年生 (大学1年生)
Second year, university	だいがく2年生 (大学2年生)
Third year, university	だいがく3年生 (大学3年生)
Fourth year, university	だいがく4年生 (大学4年生)

Talking about the year level you are in

何年生 ですか。(なんねんせい)	What year level are you in?
8年生 です。(ねんせい)	I am in Year 8.
中学2年生 です。(ちゅうがく ねんせい)	I am a second year junior high school student.

Talking about your timetable

1時かんめは 何 ですか。	What is the first period?
1時かんめは 日本語 です。	The first period is Japanese.
日本語は 何時かんめ ですか。	What period is Japanese?
日本語は 1時かんめ です。	Japanese is the first period.

三十

The negative form of です

In Japanese, to say 'not' with です, you use the phrase じゃない after the noun and before です.

1時かんめ は 日本語 ですか。	Is first period Japanese?
はい、1時かんめ は 日本語 です。	Yes, first period is Japanese.
いいえ、1時かんめ は 日本語 **じゃない** です。	No, first period is **not** Japanese.
3時かんめ は おんがく **じゃない** です。	Third period is **not** music.
しけん **じゃない** です。	It is **not** an exam.

Talking about favourite and least favourite subjects

びじゅつが 好き ですか。	Do you like art?
はい、好き です。	Yes, I like it.
いいえ、好き **じゃない** です。	No, I do not like it.

To say that you do not like a subject, say the subject then は and 好きじゃない です.

りか**は** 好き **じゃない** です。	I do not like science.
おんがく**は** 好き **じゃない** です。つまらない です。	I do not like music. It is boring.

Both 好き and にがて are な-adjectives, which means that they need な when they go before a noun.

すき**な** かもくは 何 ですか。	What is a subject that you like?
おんがく です。	Music.
好き**な** かもくは たいいく です。	A subject that I like is physical education.
にがて**な** かもくは かていか です。	A subject that I am weak at is home economics.

Saying from when until when

In Japanese, 'from' is から and 'until' is まで. You can use them together to say from one time until another time. They can also be used separately.

2時かんめは 何(なん)時 **から** ですか。	**From** what time is second period?
学校は3時半 **まで** です。	School is **until** 3.30.
ひるやすみは 何(なん)時 **から** 何(なん)時 **まで** ですか。	Lunch break is **from** what time **until** what time?
ひるやすみは 12時半 **から** 1時20分 **まで** です。	Lunch break is **from** 12.30 **until** 1.20.

だい二か

31 三十一

Find out more!
つぎは？

じっけん	experiment
べんきょう しましょう	let's study
そうじ(を) してください	please clean up
こら！	Hey!

だい二か

1.

2. いただきます！

3. ひるやすみは 何時 まで ですか。
   ええと、
   ひるやすみは 1時半 まで です。
   ああ、そう ですか。

4. まゆみさん、つぎは おんがく ですか。
   ええと…つぎは…

5. つぎは おんがく じゃない です。
   つぎは りかです。

6. ああ、いやだ！
   りかは とても つまらない です。好きじゃない です。

7. りかは おもしろい です。きょう、じっけんを します。
   ええ？
   しけん？

三十二

32

だい二か

8.
- いやだ！
- はやく、べんきょう しましょう！
- ええ？ しけん？
- しけん じゃない です。じっけん です。

9. すみません。
キ〜ン コ〜ン カ〜ン コ〜ン

10. りかは おもしろい です。

11. じゃ、みなさん。そうじを して ください。
キ〜ン コ〜ン カ〜ン コ〜ン

12.

13.
- そうじは おもしろい です！
- こら！ はやく そうじ して ください。

Comprehension questions

1. What time does the lunch break finish?
2. Explain what happened in panel 8.
3. Do you think that science is a popular subject in this school? Why or why not?

33　　三十三

My vocabulary

Essential たんご

School systems

小学校 (しょうがっこう)	primary school
中学校 (ちゅうがっこう)	junior high school
高校 (こうこう)	senior high school
大学 (だいがく)	university
何年生 (なんねんせい)	what grade
小学生 (しょうがくせい)	primary school student
中学生 (ちゅうがくせい)	junior high school student
高校生 (こうこうせい)	senior high school student

School subjects

かもく	school subjects
えい語	English
こく語	national language
すう学 (がく)	mathematics
おんがく	music
りか	science
びじゅつ	art
たいいく	PE; physical education
ぎじゅつ	technology
しゃかい	social sciences
かていか	home economics
どうとく	ethics

Talking about school timetables

～時かんめ	period
何時かんめ (なん)	What period?
～じゃない です	It is not ____
ひるやすみ	lunch break
何時 から (なん)	from what time
何時 まで (なん)	until what time
から	from
まで	until
時かんわり	timetable
そうじ	cleaning

Talking about school subjects

一ばん 好きな かもく	most favourite subject
一ばん むずかしい かもく	most difficult subject
にがてな かもく	a subject that I am weak at
むずかしい	difficult
つまらない	boring
ちょっと	little bit

Putting it all together 🔑

Introduce yourself

You are creating a new blog and you want to include an introduction about yourself supported by an audio track of you speaking. Write and record your introductory blog post. You need to include the following:

- [ ] introduction: what are you going to talk about?
- [ ] name, nationality and age
- [ ] family members
- [ ] school year level and school times
- [ ] favourite subject and least favourite subjects
- [ ] daily routine including the extra-curricular activities
- [ ] closing remarks, say thank you to those who have read or listened to your post.

だい三か
学校のたのしいイベント 3

LET'S GET STARTED!

- What kind of school events do you have on your school calendar?
- Why are school events so important?
- What are the benefits of school events? What are the disadvantages?

2 10月10日に たいいく さいが あります。

1 5月に えんそくに 行きました。
おおさか　なら　ba su　い
大阪 から 奈良 まで バスで 行きました。

3 ぶかつは すいそうがくぶ です。
まいにち れんしゅうします。

Communicating

- Talk about seasons, months and dates
- Discuss an event that you have planned on a certain date
- Talk about how you go to places
- Express how you get from one place to another

Understanding

- Read and write three *kanji*: 見, 行, 食
- Read and write dates of the month
- Use the particles に, で, から, まで, や and よ

Intercultural and cultural

- Find out about and reflect on Japanese school events
- Understand the Japanese school calendar and compare it with your own
- Compare transport that students use in Japan with your own
- Learn about ninjas.

Before you start this chapter, go to page 33 of your Activity Book.

35　三十五

My *kanji*

Try to guess the meaning of the new *kanji* in these captions using the context of the sentences and the photos.

1

te re bi　み
テレビを　見ます。

- Observe picture 1 and read the caption. Guess the meaning of 見ます.
- What do you think 行きます in picture 2 means?
- What are the girls in photo 3 about to do?
- What do you think 食べます means?

Here are the new *kanji* and new readings of some *kanji* you know for this chapter. You already know 月 in 月よう日. What do you think 三月 means?

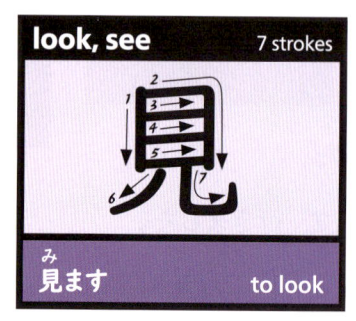

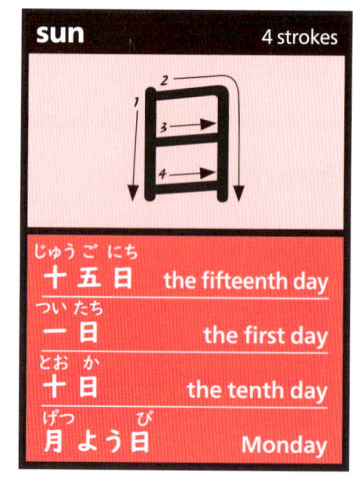

2

ba su　　　　　　　い
このバスで　えきに　行きます。

3

　　　　　　　　た
おべんとうを　食べます。
いただきます！

go — 6 strokes
行
い
行きます — to go

look, see — 7 strokes
見
み
見ます — to look

eat — 9 strokes
食
た
食べます — to eat

moon — 4 strokes
月

いち がつ		
一月		January
に がつ		
二月		February
なん がつ		
何月		what month
げつ び		
月よう日		Monday

sun — 4 strokes
日

じゅうご にち		
十五日		the fifteenth day
つい たち		
一日		the first day
とお か		
十日		the tenth day
げつ び		
月よう日		Monday

三十六

Talk time

何月？

春（はる）
三月（さんがつ）
四月（しがつ）
五月（ごがつ）

夏（なつ）
六月（ろくがつ）
七月（しちがつ）
八月（はちがつ）

秋（あき）
九月（くがつ）
十月（じゅうがつ）
十一月（じゅういちがつ）

冬（ふゆ）
十二月（じゅうにがつ）
一月（いちがつ）
二月（にがつ）

Did you notice that in Japanese you use numbers to say the months of the year? Be careful with 四月, 七月 and 九月; you must pronounce them しがつ, しちがつ and くがつ.

With a partner, practise the dialogue using the months of the year and the seasons to talk about Japan.

Then practise asking and responding according to where you live.

A 一月は ふゆ ですか。
B はい、ふゆ です。
A 八月は はる ですか。
B いいえ、なつ です。
A はるは 何月 から 何月 まで ですか。
B 三月 から 五月 まで です。

- Which months are spring, summer, autumn and winter in Japan? How different is this from where you live?
- Do you use numbers in English to say the months like in Japanese? Why do you think this is so?
- Do you know any other language that uses numbers to say the months?

はる	spring
なつ	summer
あき	autumn
ふゆ	winter
何月 (なんがつ)	which month; what month

だい三か

37   三十七

Talk time
何日ですか 🎧

The first ten days of each month, 一日 to 十日, have special readings that originate from a traditional Japanese way of counting. Look at 一日 in the calendar below. How is it read? The first day is important as it opens the new month, so it has a special name.

> You can write days of the month using *kanji* numbers (一, 二, 三) or Arabic numerals (1, 2, 3).

日	月	火	水	木	金	土
ついたち 一日	ふつか 二日	みっか 三日	よっか 四日	いつか 五日	むいか 六日	なのか 七日
ようか 八日	ここのか 九日	とおか 十日	じゅういちにち 十一日	じゅうににち 十二日	じゅうさんにち 十三日	じゅうよっか 十四日
じゅうごにち 十五日	じゅうろくにち 十六日	じゅうしちにち 十七日	じゅうはちにち 十八日	じゅうくにち 十九日	はつか 二十日	にじゅういちにち 二十一日
にじゅうににち 二十二日	にじゅうさんにち 二十三日	にじゅうよっか 二十四日	にじゅうごにち 二十五日	にじゅうろくにち 二十六日	にじゅうしちにち 二十七日	にじゅうはちにち 二十八日
にじゅうくにち 二十九日	さんじゅうにち 三十日	さんじゅういちにち 三十一日				

Practise these sentences with a partner using the calendar.

A きょうは 何日(なんにち) ですか。
B 十二日(じゅうににち) です。

何日(なんにち) which day; what day

Here are some learning strategies to help you remember the dates and months in Japanese.
- Make up your own summary of dates and months in Japanese. Write down three things that will help you to remember them.
- Use Japanese dates in your diary.

What other strategies can you think of? Discuss with a partner, and then share in class.

When you say dates in English, do they follow a regular pattern? What are the irregularities? (Hint: Compare the first three days to the rest.)

What do you notice about the readings of the dates 十一日 to 三十一日? Which dates end with か? What other patterns do you notice?

学校のカレンダー

学校のカレンダー (karendaa)

	四月	五月	六月	七月
一がっき	にゅうがくしき（4日）	はるの えんそく（25日）京都 (きょうと)		すいえい たいかい（14日）なつやすみ（7月21日〜8月31日）
	九月	十月	十一月	十二月
二がっき	あきの えんそく（20日）広島 (ひろしま)	たいいく さい（2日）	ぶんか さい（8日と9日）	ふゆやすみ（12月24日〜1月7日）
	一月	二月	三月	
三がっき			はるやすみ（3月21日〜4月7日）	

- Looking at this calendar, when does the school year start and end? When are the holidays? How is this different from or similar to your school calendar?
- What kind of school events do Australian schools have? How does this compare with Japanese schools?

Practise these sentences with a partner, referring to the school カレンダー (karendaa). Then, find out about two other events. Swap roles.

A たいいくさいは いつ ですか。
B たいいくさいは 10月2日 です。

A いつ、はるの えんそくが ありますか。
B 5月25日に はるの えんそくが あります。

[Event]は [date]です。
[Date]に [event]が あります。
p.44

にゅうがく しき	school entrance ceremony
えんそく	school excursion
すいえい たいかい	swimming carnival
やすみ	holiday
たいいく さい	sports festival
ぶんか さい	school culture festival
いつ	when

だい三か

Talk time
何で学校に行きますか 🎧

su ku u ru ba su
スクールバス

su ku u ru ba su
スクールバスで 行きます！

でんしゃで　くるまで

あるいて

あおい 中学校

じてんしゃで

ba su
バスで

ta ku shi i
タクシーで

Comprehension question
- How do the students of あおい 中学校 go to school?

With a partner, practise the dialogues.
Then, say how you go to school.
Swap roles.

A　何（なん）で 学校に 行（い）きますか。
B　でんしゃで 学校に 行（い）きます。

A　何（なん）で えきに 行（い）きますか。
B　あるいて 行（い）きます。

[Transport mode]で [place]に 行（い）きます。　p.45

What do you think で means when it is used with a mode of transport?

su ku u ru ba su スクールバス	school bus
でんしゃ	train
くるま	car
あるいて	walking; on foot
じてんしゃ	bicycle
ba su バス	bus
ta ku shi i タクシー	taxi

Many schools in Japan forbid students being driven to and from school.
You will even see small children travelling alone on public transport! How does that compare to your experience?

Check it out!
しゅうがくりょこう 🎧

These schools are going on しゅうがく りょこう, the most anticipated school trip in junior high school. Where is each school going? How do the students travel? What do they do when they get there?

1 みどり 中学校
札幌(さっぽろ) から 東京(とうきょう) まで ひこうき で 行(い)きます。原宿(はらじゅく)に 行(い)き ます。かいものを します。

2 ちゃやま 中学校
東京(とうきょう) から 広島(ひろしま) まで しんかんせんで 行(い)きます。へいわ こうえんに 行(い)きます。

3 あおい 中学校
仙台(せんだい) から 京都(きょうと) まで でんしゃで 行(い)きます。ゆうめいな おてらや じんじゃを 見(み)ます。

4 むらさき 中学校
新潟(にいがた) から 名古屋(なごや) まで バス(ba su)で 行(い)きます。おいしい とんかつを 食(た)べます。

In small groups of three or four, discuss the following.
- Have you heard of the しんかんせん?
- What is the fastest way to travel in your country?
- What do you know about the cities mentioned on the map?

しゅうがくりょこう	school trip
ひこうき	aeroplane
しんかんせん	shinkansen; bullet train
へいわ こうえん	Peace Park

Power up!
Change the ending of verb ます to たいです to express what you wish to do.

東京(とうきょう)に 行(い)きます。 → 東京(とうきょう)に 行(い)きたいです。
(I go to Tokyo.) (I want to go to Tokyo.)

とんかつを 食(た)べます。 → とんかつを 食(た)べたいです。
(I eat *tonkatsu*.) (I want to eat *tonkatsu*.)

Note the particle を often changes to が when you use this form. For example:

とんかつ**を** 食(た)べます。 → とんかつ**が** 食(た)べたいです。

p.45
[Place A]**から** [place B]**まで** [transport mode]で 行きます。

41

Check it out!
ぶんかさいのポスター

The annual school culture festival, ぶんかさい, is one of the highlights of school life. Students spend weeks to prepare for ぶんかさい. Let's see what kind of activities they do at あおい 中学校.

> What information about ぶんかさい can you find in the poster?

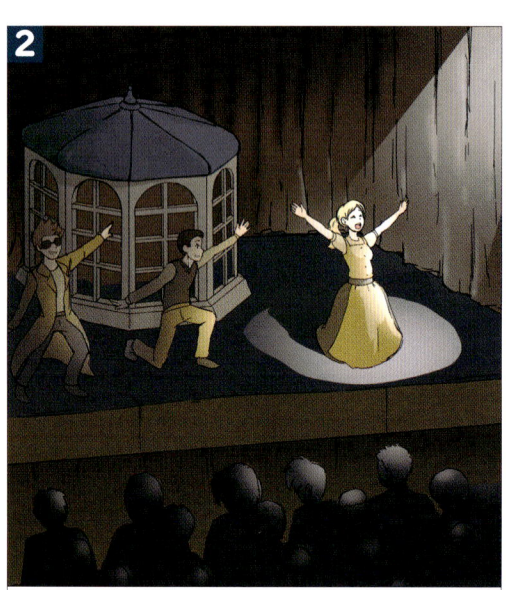

1

十月二十日（土）
十月二十一日（日）

あおい中学校の ぶんかさい

やたい！
えんげき！
ゲーム！

おいしい！
たのしい！

アクセス：えきからバスで10分

2

1年生は ミュージカル(myu u ji ka ru)を します。
見て ください！ ミュージカル(myu u ji ka ru)は 2時 から です。

3

2年生は ホットドッグ(ho t to do g gu)や おにぎりを うります。おいしいですよ。食(た)べて ください！

きて ください	please come
ミュージカル (myu u ji ka ru)	musical
見て ください	please watch
ぼくたち	we
ホットドッグ (ho t to do g gu)	hotdog
おにぎり	rice balls
うります	sell
よ	I tell you!
食べて ください	please eat

> 「ホットドッグ(ho t to do g gu)や おにぎり」
> Why do you think she used や, instead of と?
> What is the difference between や and と?

[Item 1] や [item 2] を [verb]。 p.45

だい三か

四十二　　42

Go for it!

学校のイベント 🎧

An Australian exchange student, Craig, is asking Jun about events at the Japanese school they attend.

Practise this dialogue with a partner.

Then, practise again, using the information of the other students pictured. Swap roles.

Craig
じゅんくん、すいえい たいかいは いつ ですか。

Jun
7月20日 です。

Craig
たいいくさいは いつ ですか。

Jun
9月18日 です。

Craig
ああ、そう ですか。ぶんかさいは いつ ですか。

Jun
11月4日 です。

Craig
えんそくは いつ ですか。

Jun
10月15日 です。

Craig
どこに 行きますか。

Jun
名古屋に バスで 行きます。おしろを 見ます。てんむすを 食べます。

Craig
いい ですね。

Create a similar dialogue with your partner using the dates of some of your own school events.

イベント	event

1

Name	じゅん
すいえい たいかい	20 July
たいいく さい	18 September
ぶんか さい	4 November
えんそく	15 October
	(名古屋、バス、おしろ、てんむす)

2

Name	みり
すいえい たいかい	14 July
たいいく さい	10 September
ぶんか さい	12 November
えんそく	30 November
	(京都、でんしゃ、おてら、てんぷら)

3

Name	ひろ
すいえい たいかい	19 July
たいいく さい	10 October
ぶんか さい	1 November
えんそく	24 November
	(広島、しんかんせん、へいわ こうえん、おこのみやき)

Got it?

Months

To say the months, add 月 after the number. To ask 'what month', use 何月(なんがつ).

何月(なんがつ) ですか。 — **What month** is it?
一月(いちがつ) です。 — It is **January**.

一月(いちがつ)	January	五月(ごがつ)	May	九月(くがつ)	September
二月(にがつ)	February	六月(ろくがつ)	June	十月(じゅうがつ)	October
三月(さんがつ)	March	七月(しちがつ)	July	十一月(じゅういちがつ)	November
四月(しがつ)	April	八月(はちがつ)	August	十二月(じゅうにがつ)	December

Dates

To say the day of the month (the date), you add 日 after the number for the relevant day.
To ask 'which day of the month', use 何日(なんにち).

きょうは 何日(なんにち) ですか。 — **What date** is it today?
十二日(じゅうににち) です。 — Today/It is the **twelfth**.

To ask the date of an event, you use いつ (when). You can do this in two ways.

はるの えんそくは **いつ** ですか。 — **When** is the spring excursion?
はるの えんそくは 5月25日 です。 — The spring excursion is on 25 May.
いつ、えんそくが ありますか。 — **When** is the excursion?
5月25日に えんそくが あります。 — On 25 May there is an excursion.

The particle に

土よう日**に** — **on** Saturday
一月三日(いちがつみっか)**に** — **on** 3 January
9月20日**に** 東京(とうきょう)**に** 行(い)きます。 — We are going **to** Tokyo **on** 20 September.

7時半**に** — **at** 7:30
三月(さんがつ)**に** — **in** March

The particle で and transport

You use the particle で after the mode of transport you use to go somewhere – で means 'by'. When asking 'how' or 'by what means', you use 何で.

何で 学校に 行きますか。	**How** do you go to school?
バス(ba su)で 学校に 行きます。	I go to school **by** bus.
でんしゃで	**by** train
じてんしゃで	**by** bike

When you want to say 'walking', with あるいて 行きます, you do not use で, in the same way that you do not say 'by walking' in English.

The particles から and まで

In Chapter 2 you learnt that you can use から, 'from', and まで, 'until', with expressions of time. You can also use から and まで to mean 'from' and 'to' when talking about places.

ひるやすみは 12時 **から** 1時半 **まで** です。	Lunch is **from** 12 o'clock **until** half past one. (times)
はるは 三月(さんがつ) **から** 五月(ごがつ) **まで** です。	Spring is **from** March **until** May. (months)
えき **から** 学校 **まで** バス(ba su)で 行きます。	I go by bus **from** the station **to** school. (places)

The particle や and listing many things

When you have a long list of things but do not want to list everything, in English you use expressions like 'etc.' or 'and so on' to indicate that there is more. In Japanese, you use や to say 'and so on' or 'among other things'. Compare these sentences.

ホットドッグ(ho t to do g gu)**と** おにぎりを うります。	We sell hotdogs **and** rice balls.
ホットドッグ(ho t to do g gu)**や** おにぎりを うります。	We sell hotdogs **and** rice balls, **among other things**.

The particle よ at the end of the sentence

よ is a sentence-final particle that shows the speaker's assertion about something. In English, you might say "I tell you!" or use an exclamation mark '!'.

おいしい です**よ**。	It's delicious, I tell you. / It's delicious!

Find out more!
しゅうがくりょこうに行きました 🎧

This article, written by a 中学3年生 about his しゅうがく りょこう, was put up on the school's website.

ぼくたちは 5月14日 から 17日 まで しゅうがく りょこうに 行きました。
14日に、学校 から 名古屋えき まで バスで 行きました。名古屋 から 大阪 まで しんかんせんで 行きました。

タクシーで 大阪じょうに 行きました。
大きい おしろ です。
さむらい の よろいや かたなを 見ました。
それから、おいしい すきやきを 食べました。

15日 に、大阪 から 奈良 まで でんしゃで 行きました。
奈良に しかが たくさん いました。
しかは かわいい です。
それから、だいぶつを 見ました。
とても 大きい です。

16日に、奈良から 伊賀まで バスで
行きました。伊賀に にんじゃやしきが
あります。にんじゃの うちは とても
大きい です。にんじゃの れきしを
べんきょう しました。

17日に、でんしゃと バスで
学校 まで かえりました。

Ninjas were active for a long time in Japanese history. Ninjas began their training at a very young age to gain special skills. Rather than assassinations, real ninjas did more spying and spreading groundless rumours to confuse their enemies.

They often disguised themselves as medicine men. Still now, ninjas' medicinal knowledge is handed down in some traditional medicine companies.

- Do you think that you would enjoy going on this しゅうがく りょこう? Which part would you find most interesting?
- Do you have a similar しゅうがく りょこう at your school?
- Compare the activities these 中学校 students did to the activities you would do at your school camp. What might be the same or different?

Comprehension questions

1. When was the school trip?
2. List what the students did in Osaka.
3. Where did they see deer?
4. How many and which modes of transport were used in this trip?

大阪じょう	Osaka castle
さむらい	samurai
よろい	armour
かたな	sword
すきやき	*sukiyaki*, a Japanese meat and vegetable dish that is cooked on the table
しか	deer
だいぶつ	large statue of Buddha
にんじゃ やしき	ninja house
にんじゃ	ninja

My vocabulary

Essential たんご

Seasons
春 (はる)	spring
夏 (なつ)	summer
秋 (あき)	autumn
冬 (ふゆ)	winter

School events
一学き (がっ)	Term One
二学き (がっ)	Term Two
三学き (がっ)	Term Three
にゅうがく しき	school entrance ceremony
えんそく	school excursion
すいえい たいかい	swimming carnival
やすみ	holiday(s)
はるやすみ	spring holidays
なつやすみ	summer holidays
ふゆやすみ	winter holidays
たいいく さい	school sports festival
ぶんか さい	school cultural festival
しゅうがく りょこう	school trip
ミュージカル (myuujikaru)	musical
イベント (ibento)	event
えんげき	theatre

Modes of transport
スクールバス (sukuurubasu)	school bus
でんしゃ	train
くるま	car
じてんしゃ	bicycle
バス (basu)	bus
タクシー (takushii)	taxi
ひこうき	aeroplane
しんかんせん	bullet train, Shinkansen
あるいて	walking, on foot

Question words
何月 (なんがつ)	which month; what month
何日 (なんにち)	which day; what day
いつ	when

Expressions to ask to do something
きて ください	please come
見て ください (み)	please watch
食べて ください (た)	please eat

Putting it all together

School event calendar

Create your own calendar of school events using the example on page 39 as a guide.

- ☐ draw a simple calendar using *kanji* for months
- ☐ add school events to appropriate months including dates
- ☐ add a photo or image of each event, or draw an icon

School excursion webpage

In a small group, design a webpage for a school excursion or trip you have done or wish to do.

- ☐ Be sure to include the following information: the date, the place, the transport, who you were with, what you did and what you ate.
- ☐ Include some photos to make your webpage engaging!

カタカナ

LET'S GET STARTED!

- What is the difference between *katakana* and *hiragana* characters?
- How do you think it helps if you can read *katakana* words?
- Why is it important to learn to read and write *katakana* as well as *hiragana*?

Can you guess what this sign says?

Which script is used in the red writing under the big octopus?

Manga titles can be written in *hiragana*, *katakana*, *kanji* and English.

Communicating

- Read and write names in *katakana*
- Ask and say whether you can play a particular sport or not
- Talk about the clothes you often wear
- Describe what someone is wearing
- Talk about your favourite sport and music

Understanding

- Read and write the 46 basic *katakana*
- Investigate the Japanese sound system further with *katakana*
- Read and write some popular names in *katakana*
- Learn different ways to say 'to wear'

Intercultural and cultural

- Learn more about the Japanese writing system
- Investigate the influence of other languages on Japanese
- Compare Japanese sounds with English

Before you start this chapter, go to page 49 of your Activity Book.

49　　　　　　　　　　　　　　　　　　　　　　　　　　　　　　　　　　　四十九

Katakana alphabet

Like the *hiragana* alphabet, the *katakana* alphabet has 46 characters that represent sounds and do not have a meaning on their own. Also like *hiragana*, some sounds change by adding *tenten* (゛) and *maru* (゜).

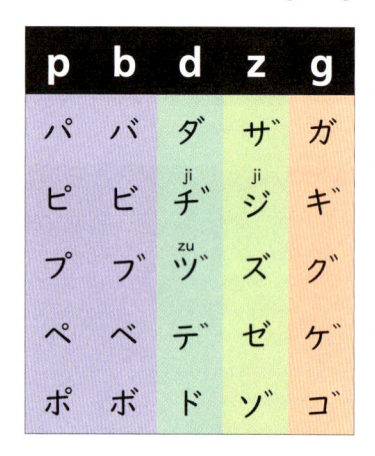

p	b	d	z	g		n	w	r	y	m	h	n	t	s	k	
パ	バ	ダ	ザ	ガ		ン	ワ	ラ	ヤ	マ	ハ	ナ	タ	サ	カ	a
ピ	ビ	ヂ(ji)	ジ(ji)	ギ				リ		ミ	ヒ	ニ	チ(chi)	シ(shi)	キ	i
プ	ブ	ヅ(zu)	ズ	グ				ル	ユ	ム	フ	ヌ	ツ(tsu)	ス	ク	u
ペ	ベ	デ	ゼ	ゲ				レ		メ	ヘ	ネ	テ	セ	ケ	e
ポ	ボ	ド	ゾ	ゴ			ヲ	ロ	ヨ	モ	ホ	ノ	ト	ソ	コ	o

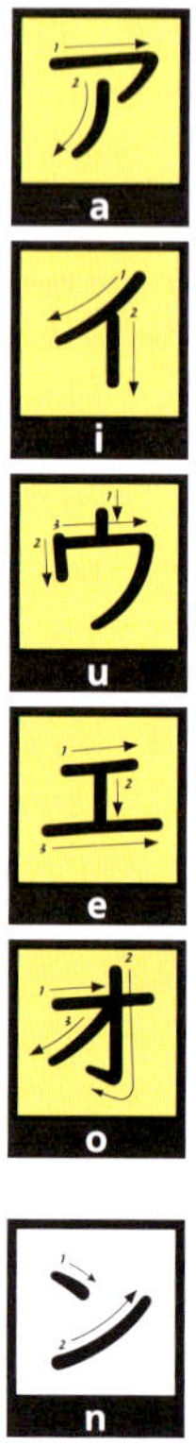

Katakana is used to write:

- words borrowed from English and other languages, such as ラーメン (ra a me n) from Chinese and インターネット (i n ta a ne t to) from English.
- generally names of people and places that are not Japanese, Chinese or Korean.
- onomatopoeic words that represent sounds or express feelings, such as 'twinkle, twinkle' キラキラ (ki ra ki ra), and a dog's bark, ワンワン (wa n wa n).
- trendy expressions or phrases: クラウド (ku ra u do) for 'cloud' and ポジティブ (po ji ti bu) for 'positive'.
- product labels and company names: Sony, ソニー (so ni), Toyota, トヨタ (to yo ta) and Uniqlo, ユニクロ (yu ni ku ro).
- the Ainu language, spoken by indigenous people and transcribed phonetically.

The vowels and 'n'

Katakana in action

Now have a go at using *katakana*. These people are asking and answering questions about their name using the 5 *katakana* vowels.

おなまえは?
アンです。
ぼくはアラン(ra)です。
わたしはエマ(ma)です。

> Look at the *Katakana* table and familiarise yourself with Japanese sound systems. How would Japanese students pronounce English names? What are the English sounds they may find hard to pronounce? You will learn combined sounds and some new special sounds in Book 3+4.

> Think about how ラー is pronounced in ラーメン. What does the bar "ー" do in *katakana* writing?

The カ(ka) & ガ(ga) lines, the サ(sa) & ザ(za) lines

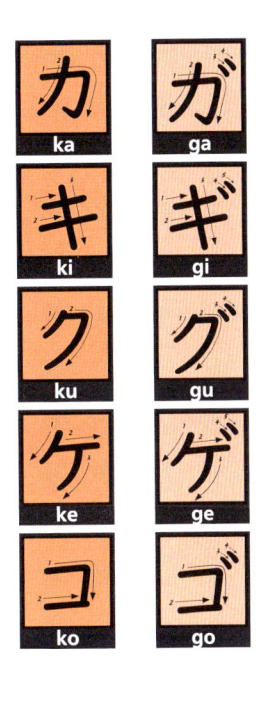

ka	ga	sa	za
カ	ガ	サ	ザ
キ ki	ギ gi	シ shi	ジ ji
ク ku	グ gu	ス su	ズ zu
ケ ke	ゲ ge	セ se	ゼ ze
コ ko	ゴ go	ソ so	ゾ zo

カタカナ

> Watch out! *Katakana* ツ (tsu) and シ (shi) look alike, so be careful not to confuse the two! The stroke order of each character will help you.

In the same way that you use a small っ in *hiragana* for double consonants, you use a small ツ(tsu) in *katakana*.

For long vowel sounds, you use the bar "ー" after the vowel sound to lengthen it. For example, car = カー, key = キー.

> When you write vertically, you write the long vowel bar vertically "|".
>
> キー   カー

Let's read!

Read the *katakana* words aloud paying attention to the small ツ and the bar "ー".

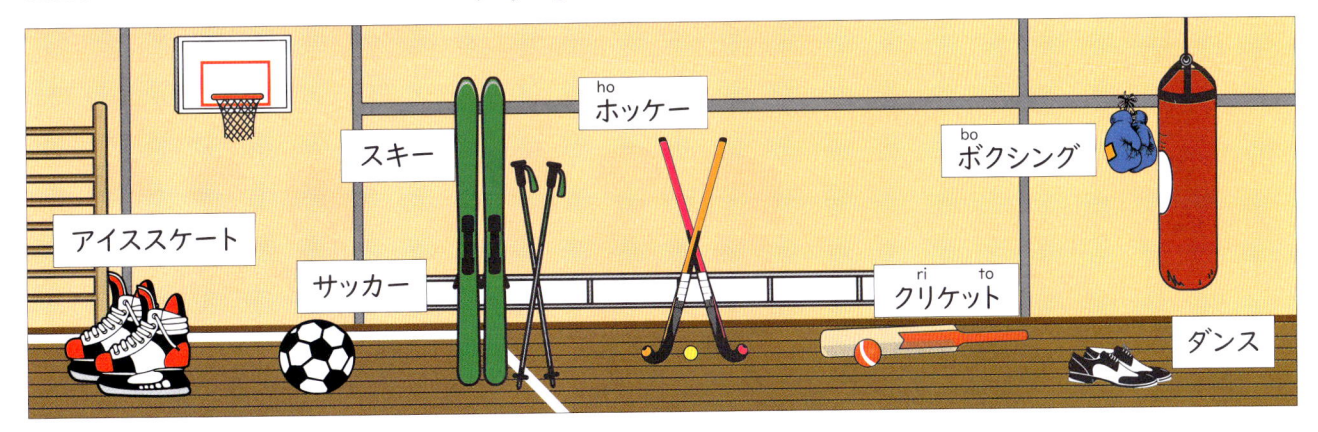

スキー
ホッケー(ho)
ボクシング(bo)
アイススケート
サッカー
クリケット(ri, to)
ダンス

Katakana in action

[Activity] が できます   p.55

できます can do/play

A スキーが できますか。
B はい、できます。
B いいえ、できません。

> Japanese use many English words in everyday conversation. What do you think オッケー(o, kke, e) means? How about サンキュー(sa, n, kyu, u)?

51   五十一

The タ & ダ lines and the ナ line

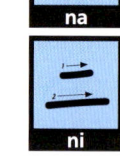

タ ta	ダ da	ナ na
チ chi	ヂ ji	ニ ni
ツ tsu	ヅ zu	ヌ nu
テ te	デ de	ネ ne
ト to	ド do	ノ no

You might have noticed that ヂ (ji) and ヅ (zu) are pronounced the same as ジ (ji) and ズ (zu), and they are rarely used in modern Japanese.

Let's read!

きます	to wear
はきます	to wear
よく	often
あまり 〜ません	not often

Labels in image:
- ネクタイ
- ハット (ha)
- ドレス (re)
- スカート
- コート
- セーター
- ジーンズ
- ソックス
- T-シャツ (sha)
- スニーカー

Katakana in action

Practise these conversations with a partner, using the above *katakana* words.

A　コートを よく きますか。
B　はい、よくきます。
C　いいえ、あまり きません。

A　よく ジーンズを はきますか。
B　いいえ、あまり はきません。
C　はい、よく はきます。

Speech bubbles:
- よく コートを きますか。
- はい、よく きます。
- いいえ、あまり きません。
- よく ジーンズを はきますか。
- いいえ、あまり はきません。
- はい、よく はきます。

Notice that two verbs are used to express 'wear'. How are they used differently?

Share your finding with your group or in class. かぶります and します are also used. かぶります is used for hat and します is also used for belt, tie, scarf and small items.

The ハ, バ & パ lines and the マ line

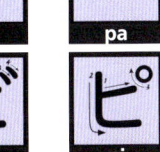

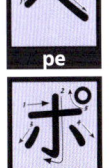

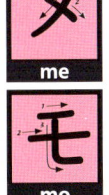

ハ ha	バ ba	パ pa	マ ma
ヒ hi	ビ bi	ピ pi	ミ mi
フ fu	ブ bu	プ pu	ム mu
ヘ he	ベ be	ペ pe	メ me
ホ ho	ボ bo	ポ po	モ mo

Let's read!

けんと
- パーカー
- マフラー
- コート
- パンツ
- ブーツ

みひろ
- ブラウス (ra)
- ネクタイ
- ベスト
- スカート
- ジャケット (ja)
- ブーツ

> パンツ is used for a pair of trousers as well as undies.

> Many of the clothing items are spelled in *katakana*. Why do you think it is? Consider how people's lives in Japan have changed over time. Can you think of any borrowed words for clothing or food items in your language? How are they spelled?

Katakana in action

A　みひろさんは 何を きて いますか。
　　みひろさんは ブラウスを きて います。
B　そして、スカートを はいて います。
　　それから、ネクタイを して います。

- Did you notice how して います was used with ネクタイ?
- What other items して います could be used for clothing items?
- How do you say 'put a ベルト on'?

The ヤ line, ラ line and ワ

ヤ ya	ラ ra	ワ wa
ユ yu	リ ri	
	ル ru	
	レ re	
ヨ yo	ロ ro	

カタカナ

Let's read!

Read this school's notice board to practise your *katakana* reading skills.

シャーロット
しゅみ
スポーツ:
ネットボール

ルーカス
しゅみ
スポーツ:
フットボール

ジョシュ
しゅみ
スポーツ:
バスケットボール

グレース
しゅみ
スポーツ:
バレエ

ロクラン
しゅみ
おんがく:
ジャズ

クロイ
しゅみ
おんがく:
Jポップ

ライアン
しゅみ
おんがく:
クラシック

オリビア
しゅみ
おんがく:
ロック

- What do you think Jポップ means? Do you know of any other type?
- Are your hobbies and/or sports on the list? If not, find the *katakana* for your hobbies and sports and add to your class board.

しゅみ	hobby/hobbies

Katakana in action

Practise this conversation with a partner, using the above *katakana* words.

A シャーロットさんの しゅみは 何 ですか。
B しゅみは スポーツ です。
A いちばん 好きな スポーツは 何 ですか。
B いちばん 好きな スポーツは ネットボール です。

You have now learnt all basic *katakana*! You will learn *katakana* special sounds in *iiTomo 3+4*.

Got it?

Asking and saying what you can and can't do

サッカーが できますか。	Can you play soccer?
はい、できます。	Yes, I can play.
いいえ、できません。	No, I can't play.

When asking questions about someone's ability to do something, you use particle が followed by できますか. できます means 'can do' or 'can play'.

Talking about what you usually or often wear

To talk about what you usually or often wear, use particle を after the clothing word, followed by the appropriate verb. よく means 'often' and can be placed before the verbs きます or はきます. To say 'not very often', use あまり before the verb ません.

コートを よく きますか。	Do you wear a coat often?
はい、よく コートを きます。	Yes, I often wear a coat.
いいえ、あまり きません。	No, I do not wear it often.

Talking about what someone is wearing at the moment

When you ask and say what clothing items someone is wearing at the moment, you use きて います or はいて います.

Remember that there is more than one way to say 'to wear'.

きます	to wear	used for clothing such as shirt, jumper and jacket, which are worn on upper or whole body
きて います	am/are/is wearing	
はきます	to wear	used for clothing such as pants, shorts, socks and shoes, which are worn on lower part of body
はいて います	am/are/is wearing	
します	to put on/wear	
して います	am/are/is putting on/ am/are/is wearing	used for accessories such as belt, brooch, necklace, ear-piercing, ring and scarf

カタカナ

My vocabulary

Essential たんご

Sports and activities

しゅみ	hobby/hobbies
スポーツ	sport(s)
サッカー	soccer
スキー	ski
ダンス	dance
クリケット	cricket
アイス スケート	ice skating
ボクシング	boxing
ネットボール	netball
フットボール	football
バスケットボール	basketball
バレエ	ballet

Talking about what you can do

(〜が)できます	I can do/play (…)
(〜が)できません	I cannot do/play (…)

Music

ジャズ	jazz
Jポップ	J-pop
クラシック	classic
ロック	rock

Clothes

T-シャツ	T-shirt	ブーツ	boots
コート	coat	マフラー	scarf
ジーンズ	jeans	ブラウス	blouse
ドレス	dress	ベスト	vest
ソックス	socks	ネクタイ	tie
セーター	jumper	ジャケット	jacket
スカート	skirt	ベルト	belt
スニーカー	sneakers	サンダル	sandals
パーカー	hoodie	カーディガン	cardigan
パンツ	pants	ハット	hat

Talking about what you wear

きます	to wear (for upper or whole body-shirts, coats, jumpers)
きて います	is wearing (for upper or whole body)
はきます	to wear (for lower part of body, from waist down – pants, jeans, socks, shoes)
はいて います	is wearing (for lower part of body, from waist down)
します	to wear (small items such as scarf, tie)
して います	is wearing (small items as above)
かぶります	to wear (for head, such as cap, hat)
かぶって います	is wearing (for head)

Putting it all together 🔑

Leisure activities in Australia

Create a survey about popular leisure activities in Japanese. Survey your class and present the findings either as a booklet or digital presentation for your sister school in Japan.

In your presentation make sure you include the following:

- ☐ headings on each page
- ☐ images
- ☐ summary of findings visually with captions in English and Japanese.

Fashion catalogue

Research popular fashion brands in Japan and create a bilingual fashion catalogue for the label. Choose your favourite brand and source its online catalogue in Japanese from the website. Download the catalogue and make it bilingual by adding English and prices in dollars.

だい四か
しゅみは何ですか

4

LET'S GET STARTED! 🎥

- Do you have any hobbies? How often do you do them?
- What would be an ideal way to spend a holiday for you?
- To what extent do hobbies help you to have a balanced lifestyle?

1 学校の やきゅうぶの メンバー です。

2 しゃしんを とります。

3 ゲームは たのしい ですね。

Communicating

- Talk about hobbies
- Discuss where and how often you do various activities
- Talk about activities you did and did not do
- Write a diary entry in Japanese

Understanding

- Read and write four *kanji*: 買, 休, 山, 川
- Investigate how to call each other within a family
- Use the particles で and に
- Learn frequency words to use to say how often you do something
- Learn how to use the verb ending 〜ませんでした

Intercultural and cultural

- Evaluate the place of homework during the summer break in Japan
- Analyse effects in the use of different scripts when referring to the same item

Before you start this chapter, go to page 61 of your Activity Book.

My kanji

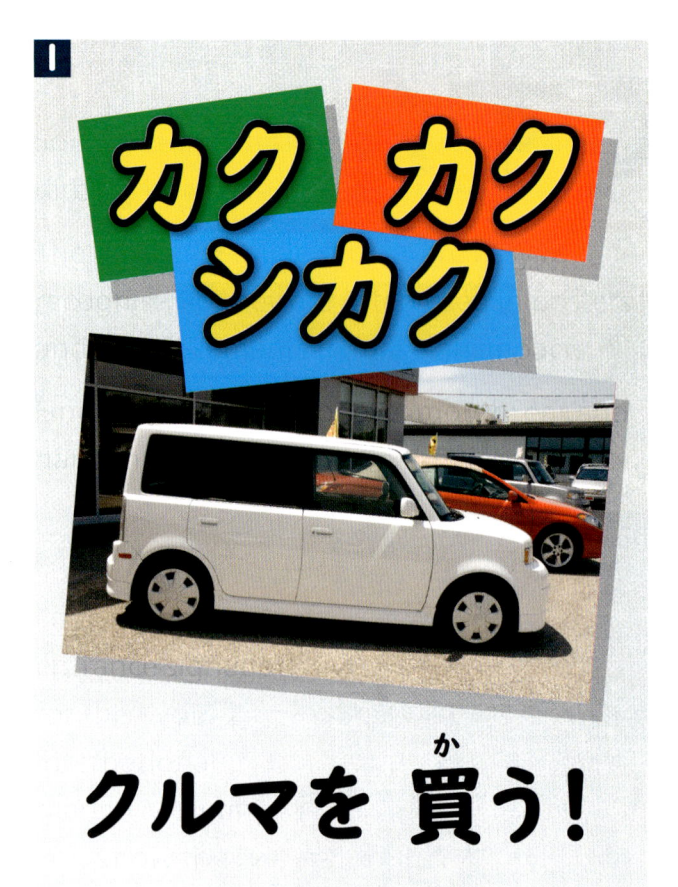

1

クルマを 買(か)う!

The word カクカク シカク at the top of the poster is written in *katakana* and means 'angular four corners'. 'Four corners' can also be written in *kanji* 四角(しかく) and in *hiragana* しかく.

- The catch-phrase on the bottom of the poster says 'I'll buy a car!'. Can you identify the *kanji* for 'buy'?
- What visual effect does the use of *katakana* and *kanji* have in this poster? Discuss with a partner.

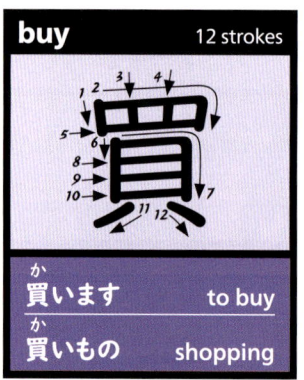

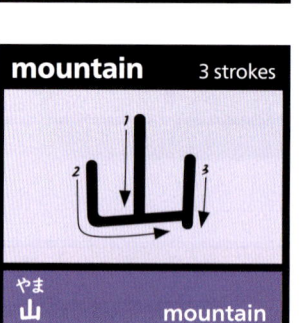

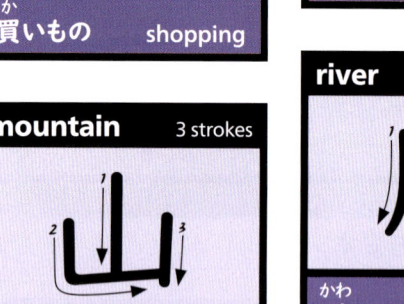

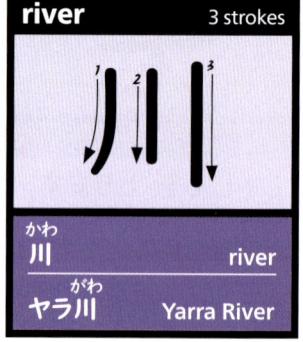

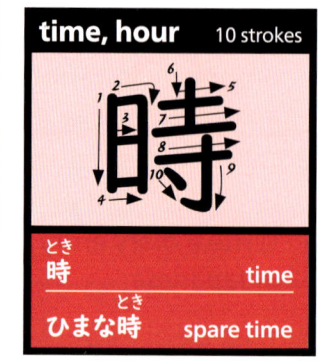

buy — 12 strokes
買
買(か)います — to buy
買(か)いもの — shopping

holiday, rest — 6 strokes
休
休(やす)み — holiday

mountain — 3 strokes
山
山(やま) — mountain

river — 3 strokes
川
川(かわ) — river
ヤラ川(がわ) — Yarra River

2

大木(おおき) ゆみこ visited a popular Japanese website where, when you type in your name, the image of a head filled with *kanji* appears. It tells you what is occupying your mind. Look at ゆみこ's results. It seems she wants a holiday. Which *kanji* shows this? What else do you think is on her mind?

Discuss with your friends how well this website might work in English.

time, hour — 10 strokes
時
時(とき) — time
ひまな時(とき) — spare time

Talk time
しゅみは何ですか

What are your hobbies? A しゅみ, or hobby, is an activity that you enjoy and pursue as an interest over a period of time.

With a partner, practise responding to しゅみは何ですか using the picture clues below.

1 スポーツ です。よく こうえんで サッカーを します。

2 りょうり です。よく うちで ケーキを つくります。

3 おんがく です。よく 学校で ギターを ひきます

4 コンピューター です。よく へやで コンピューターで あそびます。

What free time activities do you think could be called しゅみ? Why?

しゅみ	hobby
よく	often
りょうり	cooking
つくります	make
ひきます	play (an instrument)
コンピューターで	on the computer
へや	room
(で) あそびます	play (with); have fun

よく [place] で [activity] を [verb]。

p.69

Power up!
Read ゆみこ's short speech script about her hobby. Then make your own.

> しゅみは テニス です。よく 日よう日に あねと こうえんで テニスを します。テニスは ちょっと むずかしい です。でも、とても たのしい です。

だい四か

Talk time

ひまな時、何をしますか 🎧

What do you do in your spare time, your ひまな 時(とき)?

Practise asking about ひまな 時、by saying 何を しますか, and responding according to the pictures.

1 よく しゃしんを とります。
それから、ときどき えも かきます。

2 よく おんがくを ききます。
それから、ときどき ピアノも ひきます。

3 いつも けいたい でんわを つかいます。
それから、ときどき コンピューターも つかいます。

4 たいてい 山(やま)に 行きます。それから、ときどき 川(かわ)にも 行きます。

more often
いつも	always
たいてい	most of the time
よく	often
ときどき	sometimes
less often

それから、ときどき [activity 2] も [verb]。 p.69

ひまな 時	spare time
しゃしん	photo
とります	take
え	drawing; picture
かきます	draw; paint
けいたい でんわ	mobile phone
つかいます	use
山(やま)	mountain
川(かわ)	river

だい四か

六十

60

Check it out!
けいたいでんわ 🎧

1

みんな、よく けいたい でんわを つかいますか。

こんにちは。わたしは ミシェール(she)です。
きょう、けいたい でんわを 買(か)いました。
日本の けいたい でんわは おもしろい ですね。

2

お母さん

よく けいたいを つかいます。
けいたいは とても べんり ですね。

お父さん、いま、どこ？
ばんごばんは 7時半!!!
ケーキが ありますよ 👍

- Discuss the way the message is written on the mother's mobile phone.
- Discuss two different ways to write 'mobile phone', in Japanese.

3

まい日 ケータイを つかいます。
よく ブログを かきます。
ときどき テレビも 見ます。
そして、おんがくを ダウンロード します。それから、ともだちの しゃしんを とります。
ゲームも します。わたしの しゅみは ケータイ です。

ホストシスターの みゆき

- What have you noticed about the way Michelle's host mother calls her husband? Compare it with how a woman calls her husband in English.
- Compare the ways you and みゆき use mobile phones. How are they similar or different?

4

ぼくの ケータイは こども ケータイ です。
お母さんは まい日 ナビサービスを つかいます。

おとうとの ひろゆき

ひろゆき
水ようび
ごご四時半

ケータイ / けいたい	mobile phone (slang)
みんな	everyone
ブログ	blog
ダウンロード	download
ホストシスター	host sister
こども	child
ナビサービス	navigator service

だい四か

Talk time
あまり ... ぜんぜん ...

Practise saying these sentences to learn how to say 'not very often' and 'not at all' in Japanese.

1 よく 本を よみますか。
いいえ、あまり よみません。本は 好き じゃない です。

2 よく スポーツを しますか。
いいえ、あまり しません。スポーツは とくい じゃない です。

3 よく すしを つくりますか。
いいえ、ぜんぜん つくりません。りょうりは とくい じゃない です。

4 よく そうじを しますか。
いいえ、ぜんぜん しません。そうじは 好き じゃない です。

Practise talking about whether you often play sport.
When answering, pretend that you do not like any sporting activities.
Then, repeat this conversation using the activities in the table below.

	a	b	c
activity	computer game	shopping	cooking
how often	never	not very often	not very often
reason	not good at it	do not like it much	hard

p.69
あまり ... ません。
ぜんぜん ... ません。

とくい じゃない です
(I am) not good at it

しましたか？

Practise asking and answering questions about what these students did and did not do.

1. しゅうまつに スポーツを しましたか。

いいえ、しません でした。でも、いぬと さんぽを しました。

2. しゅうまつに 買いものを しましたか。

いいえ、しません でした。でも、まちで えいがを 見ました。

3. 休みに たくさん 学校の 本を よみましたか。

休みに たくさん 本を よみました。でも、学校の 本を よみません でした。

4. 休みに へやを そうじ しましたか。

いいえ。ぜんぜん そうじ しませんでした。でも、休みに インターネットで たくさん えいがを 見ました。

Compare how you form a sentence to say that you did not do something in Japanese with English.

[Verb]ました
[Verb]ませんでした

ました	did do
ませんでした	did not do
しゅうまつに	on the weekend
さんぽ	stroll; walk
休みに	during the holidays

だい四か

Check it out!
さいこうのなつ休み 🎧

だいすけ is a 小学5年生. His picture diary (えにっき) tells the story of his summer holidays (なつ休み).

1

七月二十日　木よう日　はれ

きょう から なつ休み です。やった～！
たくさん あそびます！
なつ休みが 大好き！
しゅくだいは … 八月に します。

2

七月二十一日　金よう日　はれ

かぞくと 山に 行きました。
うち から 山 まで くるまで 行きました。
ときどき、うたを うたいました。
でも、おねえちゃんは ぜんぜん
うたいません でした。

3

七月二十二日　土よう日　くもり

きょうは お父さんと 川で つりを しました。
でも、おねえちゃんは ぼくたちと
あそびません でした。
テントで ケータイで あそびました。
お母さんは カレーを つくりました。
おいしかった です。

4

七月二十三日　日よう日　はれ

きょう、おねえちゃんは ばんごはんを
つくりました。おねえちゃんの ごはんは
と～っても おいしかった です。
みんなで 川に 行きました。おねえちゃんも
行きました。きれいな ほたるを 見ました。
あしたの あさ、うちに かえります。

六十四　　　　　64

5

八月七日　月よう日　はれ

きょう、ディズニーランドで ミッキーに
あいました。
でも、スペースマウンテンに のりません
でした。

だいすけ、あした から 学校 ですよ。
なつ休みの しゅくだいを しましたか。

いいえ、しません でした。
どう しよう？

Comprehension questions

1. Does だいすけ like summer holidays?
2. Where did he go for the holidays and who with?
3. Is his mother a good cook? Use evidence from the text.
4. Why is だいすけ worrying about at the end of his holidays?
5. What can you tell about the relationships in だいすけ's family? Support your answer with his information from his diary.

- Why do you think だいすけ uses the word おねえちゃん instead of おねえさん or あね?
- と〜っても is not the usual way to write the word とても. What kind of emotion do you feel from the way the word is written? Why?

- What are the benefits of having homework during the summer break? What are the negatives? Give your opinion from different perspectives, e.g. students, parents and teachers.
- Is homework during the summer break accepted in your country? Why?

さいこう	best
えにっき	picture diary
はれ	fine (weather)
やった〜!	Yippee!
うた	song
うたいます	sing
くもり	cloudy
つり	fishing
テント	tent
おいしかった	(it) was tasty
ほたる	firefly
あした	tomorrow
あさ	morning
(に)あいます	meet (with)
(に)のります	ride (on)
どうしよう？	What should I do?

p.69

[Person]に あいます。

[Ride]に のります。

だい四か

65　　六十五

Go for it!
さいこうの休み

Jeremy and Miranda had great summer holidays. With a partner, and using the example as a guide, practise describing their holidays by saying what they did and did not do.

1

休みは どう でしたか。

休みは よかった です。うみに 行きました。そして、まい日 ビーチで ざっしを よみました。それから、たくさん 買いものを しました。でも、ぜんぜん べんきょう しません でした。さいこうの 休み でした。

- ✓ うちに いました。
- ✓ コンピューターで あそびました。
- ✓ えを かきました。
- ✗ そうじ しました。

2

3

- ✓ まちに 行きました。
- ✓ えいがを 見ました。
- ✓ 本を よみました。
- ✗ べんきょう しました。

Ask at least three people about their best holidays. さいこうの 休みは? Copy the table below into your notebook and take notes in Japanese.

なまえ	行きました	しました	しません でした

Power up!
Now describe one of your classmate's best holiday in Japanese in your notebook.

どう でしたか	How was it?
よかった です	… was good
うみ	sea; ocean
ビーチ	beach
うちに います	stay at home

六十六

66

しゅみは？

Emma is asking Masato, an exchange student, about his interests. With a partner, role-play the conversation. Then, have a go at making it your own.

エマ
まさとくん、しゅみは 何 ですか。

まさと

| ぼくの しゅみは | どくしょ
スポーツ
りょうり | です。 | まい日
よく | 本を よみます。
バスケットボールを します。
ケーキを つくります。 |

エマ

| じゃ、 | ときどき | まんがも よみますか。
テニスも しますか。
すしも つくりますか。 |

まさと

| いいえ、 | あまり
ぜんぜん | まんがを よみません。
テニスを しません。
すしを つくりません。 | まんがは
テニスは
すしは | 好き じゃない です。
とくい じゃない です。 |

エマ
そう ですか。

まさと
エマさんは しゅうまつに 何を しましたか。

エマ

| 本を よみました。 | でも、 | ぜんぜん | テレビを 見ません でした。
ケータイを つかいません でした。
買いものに 行きません でした。 |

まさと
えっ、 どうして ですか。

エマ

| きょう | えい語の テストが
ピアノの レッスンが
テニスの しあいが | ありました。 だから | べんきょう しました。
れんしゅう しました。 |

まさと
へぇ、かわい そう。

どくしょ	reading (as a hobby)
どうして	why
テスト	test

レッスン	lesson
しあい	games; match
かわいそう	poor thing

Got it?

Talking about hobbies

しゅみは 何 ですか。	What is your hobby?
（しゅみは）スポーツ です。	(My hobby is) sport.
（しゅみは）りょうり です。	(My hobby is) cooking.

To make it clear whose hobby you are talking about, add the person's name and の before しゅみ.

お父さん**の** しゅみは 何 ですか。	What is your father**'s** hobby?
父**の** しゅみは つり です。	My father**'s** hobby is fishing.

To say that you really like a certain hobby, you would use the expression 〜が 大好き です.

つり**が** 大好き です。	I really like fishing.

Saying how often you do something

When talking about an activity that you do, you may want to give information about how often you do it.

よく 本を よみますか。	Do you **often** read books?
はい、**よく** よみます。	Yes, I **often** read.
ときどき よみます。	I **sometimes** read.
いいえ、**あまり** よみ**ません**。	No, I do **not** read **very often**.

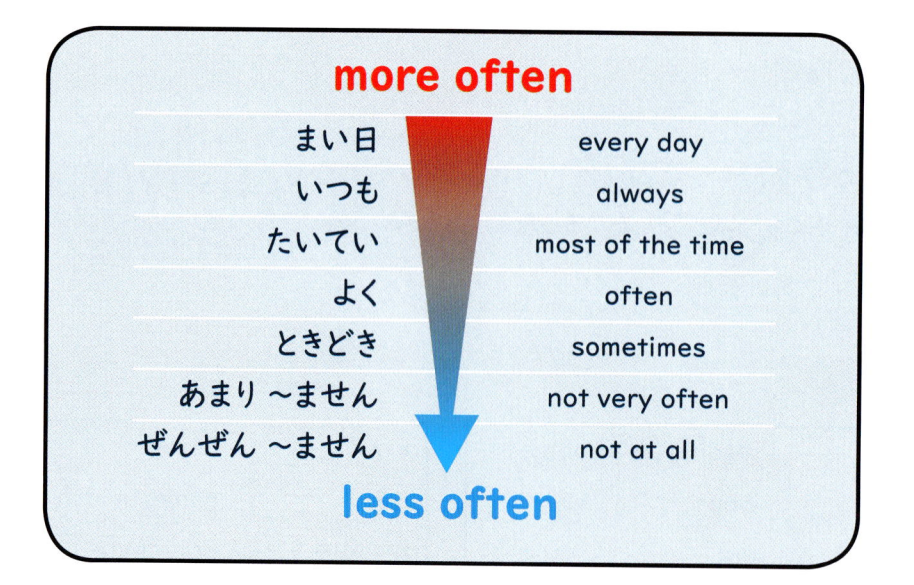

more often

まい日	every day
いつも	always
たいてい	most of the time
よく	often
ときどき	sometimes
あまり 〜ません	not very often
ぜんぜん 〜ません	not at all

less often

まい日 けいたいを つかいます。	I use a mobile phone **every day**.
よく けいたいを つかいます。	I **often** use a mobile phone.
ときどき けいたいを つかいます。	I **sometimes** use a mobile phone.
あまり けいたいを つかい**ません**。	I do **not** use a mobile phone **very often**.
ぜんぜん けいたいを つかい**ません**。	I do **not** use a mobile phone **at all**.

あまり must be used in a sentence that ends with a negative form, such as 〜ません or 〜ない です. あまり (or あんまり) means 'not very often' or 'not very much'.

いいえ、**あまり** よみ**ません**。	No, I do **not** read a book **very often**.
本は **あまり** 好き **じゃない** です。	I do **not** like books **very much**.

Saying what you did not do

You learnt that the verb ending 〜ません is used to say 'I do not do —'. To talk about something that you did not do in the past, use the verb ending 〜ません でした.

休(やす)みに 学校の 本を よみ**ません**。	I **do not** read school books in the holidays.
休(やす)みに 学校の 本を よみ**ません でした**。	I **did not** read school books in the holidays.
そうじを し**ません でした**。	I **did not** do the cleaning.

The particle で

To say that you do an action in or at a place, use the particle で after the place noun.

よく こうえん**で** サッカーを します。	I often play soccer **in** the park.

The particle に

The particle を is used before most verbs; however, some verbs require the particle に. To meet someone, あいます, is one of them.

ミッキー**に** あいました。	I met Mickey (Mouse).

In this example, you cannot use 見ます. 見ます is the verb 'to see', and it means that you just saw someone but did not talk!

You also use に when saying 'taking a ride'.

スペースマウンテン**に** のりました。	I rode on Space Mountain.

Find out more!
日本に行きます！

ジェニファー won an essay contest held by a Japanese tour company and received a return ticket to Japan as a prize.

1. 見て、見て！

2. なつ休みに 日本に 行きます。 — え？ きょ年も 行きましたね。

3. ええ。でも、あきはばらに 行きません でした。

4. だから、こんどは アニメグッズを たくさん 買います。

5. いい ですねぇ～。日本で どこに とまりますか。 — ええと...。まさしくんの おばあさんの うち です。

6. まさしくん、おばあさんは 何さい ですか。 — 65さい です。でも、とても げんき ですよ。

7. おばあさんの しゅみ は 何 ですか。おみやげを 買います。

8. おばあさんの しゅみは スポーツと コンピューター です。 — スポーツと コンピューター？ かっこいい ですね。

Comprehension questions

1 Describe まさし's relationship with his grandmother. Support your answer with information from the story.
2 How is his grandmother portrayed?

見て！	Look!
きょ年	last year
こんど	this time
アニメグッズ	animation goods/merchandise
（に）とまります	stay (at)
げんき（な）	fit
チャット	chat
ぼうし	hat
いい ですね	sounds good
ドキドキ	an onomatopoeic expression implying nervousness and excitement
どんな 人 かな？	I wonder what he/she is like.

My vocabulary

Essential たんご

Free time activities

しゅみ	hobby
りょうり	cooking
(ケーキ/すし)を つくります	make (cake/sushi)
(ギター/ピアノ)を ひきます	play (guitar/piano)
(で)あそびます	play (with); have fun (with)
しゃしんを とります	take photos
えを かきます	draw a picture
(けいたいでんわ)を つかいます	use (a mobile phone)
さんぽを します	have a walk
うたを うたいます	sing a song
(person)に あいます	meet a person
(ride)に のります	to ride on
うちに います	stay at home
(place)に とまります	stay at
どくしょ	reading (as a hobby)
つり	fishing
とくいじゃないです	(I am) not good at it

Places

へや	room	やま 山	mountain
うみ	sea; ocean	かわ 川	river
ビーチ	beach		

Frequency words

いつも	always
たいてい	most of the time
よく	often
ときどき	sometimes
あまり 〜ません	not very often
ぜんぜん 〜ません	not at all

Time words

ひまな 時(とき)	spare time
しゅうまつに	on the weekend
休(やす)みに	during the holidays
あした	tomorrow
あさ	morning
きょ年(ねん)	last year

Talking about a past holiday

(verb)ました	did
(verb)ませんでした	did not do
どう でしたか。	How was it?
よかった です	… was good
はれ	fine (weather)
くもり	cloudy

Putting it all together 🔑

Spare time activities now and then

Conduct a survey with ten teenagers on how they spend their free time and how their parents spent their free time in their teens. You must ask what they often do, sometimes do, do not do very often and do not do at all. You can ask questions in English. Compile the results in Japanese using a chart and/or graph either on paper or using a multimedia program. Then present it to your class.

When presenting the results to the class, use the correct tenses.

'Best ever holiday' diary

Write a えにっき (picture diary) using your own photos and/or images from magazines and the internet to illustrate what happened on your 'best holiday'. Present it on paper, such as in a journal or as a large poster, or using a multimedia program. You must include:

- [ ] a heading: さいこうの 休み
- [ ] the date, day of the week and the weather
- [ ] where you went
- [ ] what you did and with whom
- [ ] what it was like
- [ ] what you did not do and why

だい五か
どんなキャラクターですか 5

LET'S GET STARTED!
- What do you know about Japanese anime or manga?
- Why do you think anime and manga have gained popularity outside Japan?
- Are anime and manga only for children?

2 かわいい キャラクター ですね。

3 ドラえもんは とても ゆうめい です。

1 かっこいい 人 ですね。

Communicating
- Talk about physical appearance
- Discuss personality and abilities
- Talk about your favourite anime and manga characters

Understanding
- Read and write four *kanji*: 目, 口, 耳, 手
- Build up a passage using conjunctions effectively
- Use the て-form of い-adjectives and な-adjectives
- Create the past negative tense of verbs

Intercultural and cultural
- Explore how anime and manga are used in Japanese society
- Recognise Akihabara as a popular destination for anime and manga fans

Before you start this chapter, go to page 79 of your Activity Book.

My kanji
Parts of the body

だい五か

Some of the *kanji* for body parts were directly developed from pictures.

These *kanji*'s simple shapes are easy to recognise, so they are often used in posters and advertisements to make an impact.

Find the characters for eye, mouth, ear and hand in the illustration on the right.

Look at the entrance signage for the Kyoto International Manga Museum. You know the second *kanji* for 'mouth'. What do you think the first *kanji* means to make the word 'entrance'?

eye	5 strokes
目	
め 目	eye
め 目が 大きい	big eyes

mouth	3 strokes
口	
くち 口	mouth
くち 口が 小さい	small mouth

ear	6 strokes
耳	
みみ 耳	ear
みみ 耳が 大きい	big ears

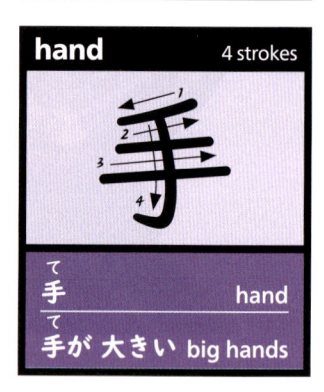

hand	4 strokes
手	
て 手	hand
て 手が 大きい	big hands

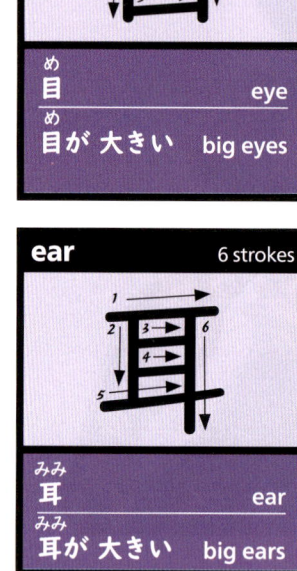

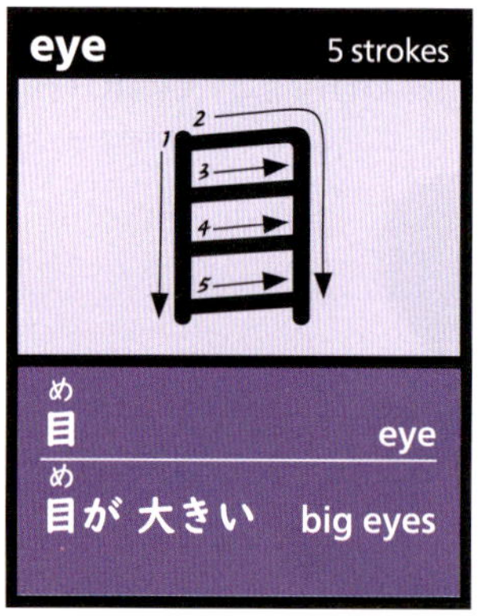

What do you think the cover of this book 英語耳 (えいごみみ) is telling its readers?

> Discuss in groups the effectiveness of the picture and the *kanji* on the cover.

person	2 strokes
人	
ひと 人	person
どんな 人(ひと)	what type of person?

七十四

74

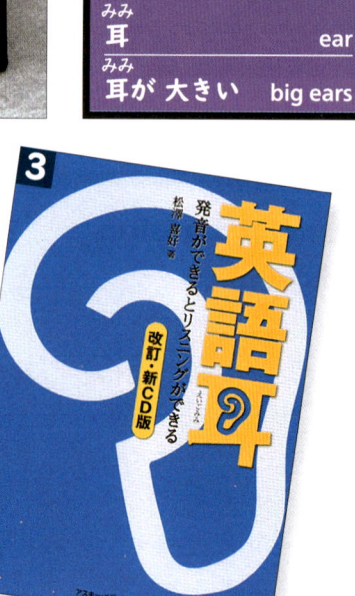

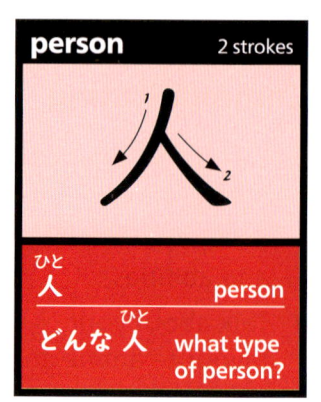

Talk time
どんなかおですか

You have probably heard of アニメ and まんが. The word アニメ is an abbreviation of animation and refers to animated films. You might also hear the word ジャパニメ. What do you think it means?

まんが (漫画) are Japanese comic books. まんが have a style that differs from French or American comics; the physical features of まんが characters are often less realistic.

Practise answering the question どんな かお ですか to describe these アニメ characters.

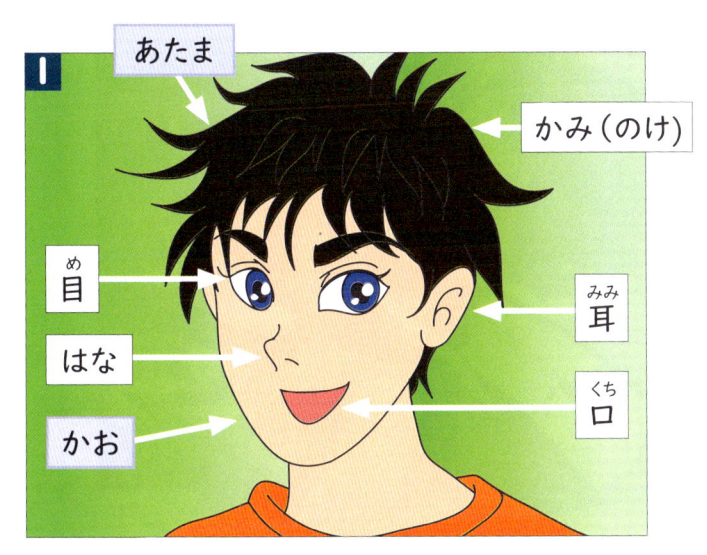

1
- あたま
- かみ（のけ）
- 目 (め)
- 耳 (みみ)
- はな
- 口 (くち)
- かお

2
ピカチュウは 耳が 大きい です。
そして、はなが 小さい です。

3
ポニョは かみが ながい です。
そして、目が かわいい です。

4
トトロは 目が 小さい です。
でも、口が 大きい です。

5
ケニーは かみが みじかい です。
そして、はなが 小さい です。

アニメ	anime
まんが	comic book; cartoon
ながい	long
みじかい	short

[Name]は [body part]が [adjective]です。

p.81

75 　 七十五

だい五か

Talk time

どうして好きですか 🎧

Pretend that these are your favourite characters. With a partner, practise reading aloud to say why you like each character in pictures 1 and 2, and then have a go at doing it for pictures 3 and 4.

1 ナツ・ドラグニル

この人(ひと)は せが 高(たか)い です。
そして、あしが ながい です。
それから、目(め)が すてき です。
だから、大好(だいす)き です。

2 悟飯(ごはん)

悟飯(ごはん)は せが ひくい です。
そして、目(め)も 口(くち)も 大きい です。
それから、あしが みじかい です。
でも、やさしい です。
そして、とても つよい です。
だから、わたしは 悟飯(ごはん)が 好き です。

3 ミーナ

4 サウザー

せが たかい	tall (height)
あし	leg; foot
やさしい	nice; gentle; kind
すてき(な)	nice; gorgeous
せが ひくい	short (height)
つよい	strong
しっぽ (があります)	(has a) tail

第五か / 七十六 / 76

Check it out!

ドラえもんはさいこう！

Read what ゆか writes about her favourite まんが character, ドラえもん.

ドラえもん

1 わたしの かぞくは みんな ドラえもんの ファン です。

ドラえもんは ねこの ロボット です。ドラえもんは せが ひくい です。手も あしも みじかい です。でも、かわいい です。それに、ドラえもんは とても やさしい です。ドラえもんは 耳が ありません。ねずみが 食べました。

2 おとうとの 好きなゲーム です。先しゅう、わたしは 父と このゲームを しました。父は じょうずに できました。でも、わたしは ぜんぜん できませんでした。

3 母は よく コーヒー をのみます。

4 どらやき

九月三日は ドラえもんの たんじょう日
ドラえもんは どらやきが 大好き です。
おいしい ですよ。母も わたしも 大好き です。

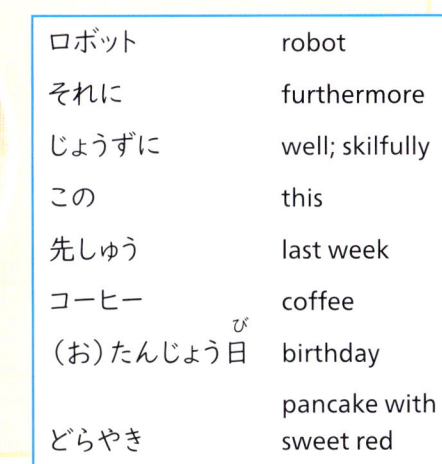

ロボット	robot
それに	furthermore
じょうずに	well; skilfully
この	this
先しゅう	last week
コーヒー	coffee
（お）たんじょう日	birthday
どらやき	pancake with sweet red bean paste

Comprehension questions

1. What do we know about ドラえもん?
2. How do we know that ドラえもん appeals to a wide range of people?
3. What year was ドラえもん born?

Discuss how まんが characters are used in your daily life in Australia. Is it similar to or different from Japan?

Talk time
好きなキャラクターはどんな人？ 🎧

What is your favourite キャラクター like? Look at the images and descriptions below to learn how to describe things using more than one adjective.

Practise reading these sentences aloud.

1. つよくて かっこいい です。
2. やさしくて きれい です。
3. へんで おもしろい です。
4. きれいで かっこいい です。

With a partner, practise combining adjectives by dropping the final い and adding くて to the first adjective if it is a い-adjective or dropping the な and adding で for the first adjective if it is a な-adjective. Use the descriptions below.

1. かみが ながい　かわいい
2. 目が 小さい　おもしろい
3. しずか（な）　つよい
4. 目が すてき（な）　かわいい

[い-adjective] くて + [adjective]
[な-adjective] で + [adjective]
p.81

へん（な）　strange

七十八　78

Check it out!

Look at the photo story ミシェール[she] created to show that アニメ and まんが is everywhere in Japan.

みなさんは アニメと まんがが 好き ですか。日本では いろいろなところに アニメや まんがが あります。

1 でんしゃの マナー

きのう、でんしゃで ちょっと へんで おもしろい ポスターを 見ました。どっちが へん ですか。

2 くまモン、キュート!

くまモンは 日本の 熊本県[くまもとけん]の マスコット キャラクター です。あしが みじかくて かわいい です。日本じゅうで にんきが あります。いろいろなグッズも あります。

3 何[なん]の本?

この本は とても むずかしいか学の本 です。でも、まんがで べんきょう します。だから、べんきょうが たのしい ですよ。

4

フランスから きました!

ブラジルから きました!

日本の まんがと アニメは すごい ですね。

コスプレ です。まい年[とし]、名古屋[なごや]で イベントが あります。みんな かっこよくて すてき ですね。

Comprehension questions

1. What motivates Michelle to make this photo story?
2. How does Michelle analyse the popularity of Kumamon?
3. What impact did the books with まんが cover have on her?

- What do you think is special about the place アニメ and まんが have gained in Japanese society?
- Have you noticed any influences of Japanese アニメ and まんが in your daily life?

ところ	place	日本中[じゅう]	all over Japan	いろいろな	various	きました	came
どっち	which one	にんきが あります	popular	グッズ	goods; merchandise	コスプレ	cosplay
熊本県[くまもとけん]	Kumamoto Prefecture			か学	science	まい年[とし]	every year
						イベント	event

79

Go for it!
どれが 好き？

けんじ would like to be a まんがか (cartoonist) in the future. He is showing a friend some of the characters for his latest まんが. Which one do you like? Why?

どれが 好き？

Give a short speech to the class describing your favourite まんが character. Below is an example. Include more information to describe your choice convincingly.

わたしの 好きな キャラクターは ゆきや です。ゆきやは せが 高い です。かみが みじかい です。目が 大きくて すてき です。わたしは きれいな 目が 好き です。ゆきやは からてが とくい です。ゆきやは つよくて かっこいい です。だから、ゆきやが 好き です。

2 らいら
- 15さい
- スポーツが とくい
- よく 本を よみます

1 ゆきや
- 13さい
- からてが とくい
- すう学が にがて

3 たいしょう
- らいらの 父
- とても つよくて ちょっと こわい

4 ぴょんきち
- にんじんが 好き
- ねこが こわい

| どれ | which one? |
| にんじん | carrot |

Got it?

Describing appearances

[Person]は [body part]が [adjective]です。 　p.73

ポニョは 目が 大きい です。 　　　　Ponyo has big eyes.

You can use も to mean 'also'. Place it instead of が, after the body part.

そして、口も 大きい です。 　　　　And she **also** has a big mouth.

If you are talking about two body parts, use も after each to indicate 'and' or 'also'.

目も 口も 大きい です。 　　　　Her eyes **and** her mouth are big.

To emphasise a contrast, such as between something big and something small, use は instead of が.

目が 大きい です。でも、口は 小さい です。 　The eyes are big. However, the mouth is small.

Describing with more than one adjective

To list or join two adjectives in English you use 'and'. In Japanese, to join い-adjectives, you use the form for the first adjective. To make the て-form of an い-adjective, drop the last い and add くて.

ゆきやは **つよくて かっこいい** です。 　Yukiya is **strong and cool**.

To make the て-form of な-adjectives, replace な in the first adjective with で.

ケニーは **へんで おもしろい** です。 　Kenny is **strange and interesting**.

Which one? Which? What kind of?

どっち(どちら) is used to say 'which one (of the two)'. どれ is also used for 'which one' when there are three or more items. どの is used before an item or a person to ask 'which item/person'. どんな means 'what kind of' and is used to get more detailed information what is being discussed.

どっち(どちら) ですか。	Which one (of the two) is it?	どの 人 ですか。	Which person is it?
どれ ですか。	Which one (of the three or more) is it?	どんな まんが ですか。	What kind of *manga* is it?

だい五か

Find out more!
あきはばらはおもしろくてたのしい！

1. ここは あきはばら です。

2. 日本の アニメも ゲームも せかい中で にんきが あります。日本の ゲームは たのしくて おもしろい です。

3. 日本の アニメが 好き ですか。

大好き です。日本の アニメは ちょっと へん です。でも、とても おもしろい です。

4. 何を 買いましたか。

コスプレの ふく です。ちょっと へんで おもしろい です。でも、好き です。

5. よく まんがきっさに きますか。

はい。よく きます。

6. ここに まんがが たくさん あります。あたらしい まんがも ふるい まんがも あります。

Comprehension questions

1 How is Akihabara portrayed in the story? What did you learn about Akihabara?
2 What do you think is special and interesting about manga cafés?

Would you find it relaxing or enjoyable to spend all day at a manga café? Why? Or Why not?

ここ	this place; here
せかい中で	all over the world; worldwide
ふく	clothes
まんがきっさ	manga café
きます	come
オンラインゲーム	online game
サービス	service

My vocabulary

Essential たんご

Body parts

あたま	head	くち	mouth
かお	face	て	hand(s)
かみ(のけ)	hair	せ	body height
目(め)	eye(s)	あし	leg(s); foot
耳(みみ)	ear(s)	しっぽ	tail
はな	nose		

Adjectives

ながい	long
みじかい	short
(せが)たかい	tall (height)
(せが)ひくい	short (height)
つよい	strong
すてき(な)	nice; gorgeous
へん(な)	strange

Useful vocabulary and expressions

それに	furthermore
どれ	which one (of the three or more)
にんきが あります	popular
せかい中(じゅう)で	all over the world; worldwide
アニメ	anime (animated film)
キャラクター	character
グッズ	goods; merchandise
コスプレ	cosplay
ふく	clothes
まんがきっさ	manga café

Additional vocabulary

サービス	service	(お)たんじょう日(び)	birthday
まんがか	cartoonist	どらやき	pancake with sweet red bean paste
この	this		
ここ	here	にんじん	carrot
きます	come	か学(がく)	science
ロボット	robot	まい年(とし)	every year
とけい	clock; watch	イベント	event
先しゅう	last week	じょうずに	well; skilfully
コーヒー	coffee	いろいろな	various
ところ	place		

Putting it all together

Designing a new hero/heroine

Create a new hero/heroine and present it to the class in a multimedia or poster format.

In your presentation you must include:

- ☐ image/drawing of an original hero/heroine
- ☐ hero's/heroine's name and age
- ☐ description of the physical appearance, personality and abilities in Japanese

When presenting:

- ☐ begin by addressing the class: みなさん、みて ください。これが あたらしい ヒーロー/ヒロイン です。
- ☐ finish your presentation with a closing: これで おわり です。ありがとう ございました。

Creating a self-promo video

You have decided to audition for a role in a film based on a Japanese manga. Create a self-promo video to send to the production team.

In your video you must include:

- ☐ your name and age
- ☐ description of your physical appearance, personality and abilities
- ☐ why you want to get the specific role.

Make sure that you use persuasive language such as そして、それに and とても, with clear speech and effective use of tone to convince the production team that you are the best choice for the role.

だい六か
おまつりとおいわい

6

LET'S GET STARTED! 📹

- How do you celebrate birthdays?
- How do your local festivals reflect Australian culture?
- To what extent are traditional festivals beneficial to young people?

はなび です。 きれい ですね！

ともだちと　おまつりに　行きます。

だいちくんの　たんじょう日（び） です。

Communicating
- Say happy birthday
- Explain how you celebrate your birthday
- Talk about what you received on your birthday
- Discuss what you did on a special occasion

Understanding
- Use the particles に, から and を
- Say what you received using the past tense of もらいます
- Say 'do it together'
- Use the particle で with みんな to mean 'all together'

Intercultural and cultural
- Compare how people celebrate their birthdays and festivals in Japan and in Australia
- Learn about important birthdays in Japan
- Understand historical meanings of festivals
- Discover what you can find and buy in Japanese festivals

Before you start this chapter, go to page 91 of your Activity Book.

85　　　　　　　　　　　　　　　　　　　　　　　　八十五

Talk time
おたんじょう日おめでとう！ 🎧

What do you do on your birthday? With a partner, practise saying these sentences in response to the question たんじょう日に 何を しますか.

1. たんじょう日に ドレスを きます。

2. おたんじょう日 おめでとう！ ありがとう！
たんじょう日に パーティーを します。

3. たんじょう日に ケーキを 食べます。

4. たんじょう日に うたを うたいます。

5. たんじょう日に みんなで おいわい します。

ドレス	dress
きます	wear (clothes)
みんなで	everyone together
パーティー	party
おいわい します	celebrate

[Occasion]に [item/activity]を [verb]。 p.93

八十六　　　　　　　　　　　　　　　86

たんじょう日に何をもらいましたか

What did you receive on your birthday? With a partner, practise asking たんじょう日に 何を もらいましたか and responding with the sample sentences given.

1 しょうくん から（or に）ゲームを もらいました。

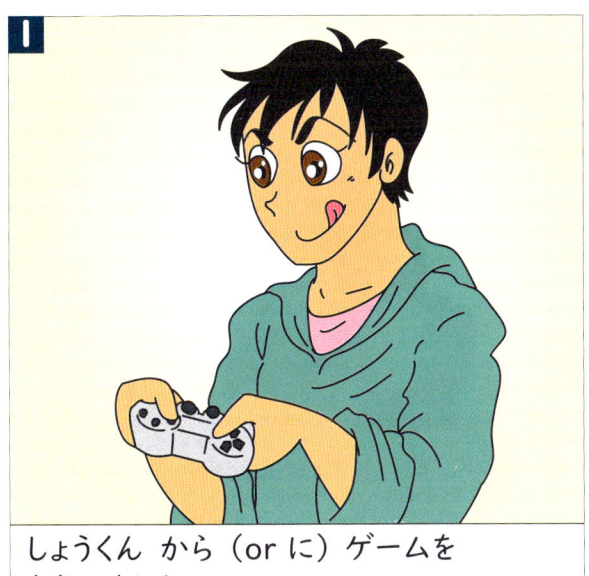

2 あやさん から（or に）プレゼントを もらいました。

3 父から（or に）ギフトカードを もらいました。

4 母から（or に）本を もらいました。

What are the two particles which mean 'from' in these sentences?

もらいます	receive
プレゼント	present; gift
ギフトカード	gift card

[Person]から（or に）[item]を もらいました。

Traditionally in Japan, it is considered bad manners to open a gift in front of the person who gave it to you. This is changing as young people are influenced by Western media. It is best to ask あけて もいいですか (May I open it?) before you open the gift.

Power up!
With a partner, have a go at saying what you received on your birthday. Your partner listens and translates. Swap roles.

Check it out!

みゆさんとゆうまくんのたんじょう日 🎧

Two Japanese high school students are writing about their recent birthday celebrations.

1

みゆ です。15さい です。わたしの たんじょう日は 4月3日 です。学校で ともだち から プレゼントを もらいました。それから、みんなで カラオケに 行きました。たのしかった です。

2

よる、かぞくと レストランに 行きました。おいしい ハンバーグを 食べました。そして、大きい ケーキを 食べました。

3

ゆうま です。13さい です。中学2年生 です。ぼくの たんじょう日に そふと そぼが うちに きました。

4

ばんごはんは すしと とんかつと ケーキ です。ぼくは すしと とんかつが 大好き です。母の りょうりは とても おいしかった です。

Comprehension questions

1 What did みゆ do on her birthday?
2 What did ゆうま do on his birthday?
3 Do you think that both had a good birthday? Why?

たのしかった です	it was fun
よる	night; evening
レストラン	restaurant
おいしかった です	it was delicious

- What do you do on your birthday? How does this compare with what みゆ and ゆうま do on their birthdays?
- What would be your ideal birthday celebration?

Power up!

In small groups, have a go at saying what you did on your last birthday using the above as model. Then present each other's celebrations to the class.

八十八

Talk time
おまつりに何をしますか 🎧

With a partner, practise asking おまつりに 何を しますか and responding according to the clues.

おまつりに 何を しますか

1. はっぴを きます。
2. はなびを 見ます。
3. わたあめを 食べます。
4. おめんを 買います。

はっぴ	a traditional coat worn at festivals; a *happi* coat
はなび	fireworks
わたあめ	fairy floss
おめん	mask

What do you do at festivals? Compare with the activities listed here. Do you wear special clothes like a *happi* coat? What kind of special food do you eat? What are the historical meanings to these special clothes and foods?

だい六か

八十九

Check it out!

おまつりに行きました

Michael, an Australian student, is staying with a host family in Kyoto and attending school in Japan with his host brother りくと.
For a school assignment he wrote about his first experience of a festival in Japan.

1

7月17日に、ぎおんまつりに 行きました。ぎおんまつりは ゆうめいな
京都(きょうと)の おまつり です。

2

でんしゃで 行きました。
でんしゃは とても こんで いました。
京都(きょうと)の まちは もっと こんで いました。

3

きれいな ほこが たくさん ありました。
ほこの おんがくを ききました。
めずらしい おんがく でした。おとこの人が
おんがくを えんそう します。おんなの人は
しません。おもしろい ですね。

4

やたいが たくさん ありました。たこやきや とうもろこしを 食べました。そして、やきとりを 食べました。つめたい おちゃを のみました。おなかが いっぱい！

5

それから、はなびを 買いました。そして、また でんしゃで うちに かえりました。とても おもしろかった です。

Comprehension questions

With a partner, answer these questions.

1. How (type of transport) did they go to the festival and return home?
2. What was Michael's impression of the transport they used and the city of Kyoto?
3. What did they eat at the festival?
4. What did you learn about the Gion festival from Michael?

- Do you think that the Gion festival is traditional or modern? Why?
- Do you have a festival similar to the Gion festival? What about in other countries?
- What are the differences between festivals you celebrate and the Gion festival? What does it show about the differences between your culture and Japan's?

こんで いました	it was crowded
もっと	more
ほこ	portable shrine
めずらしい	unusual
おとこの 人	man; men
えんそう します	play; perform (musical instruments)
おんなの 人	woman; women
やたい	stall
たこやき	octopus dumplings
とうもろこし	corn (on the cob)
つめたい	cold
おなかが いっぱい！	I'm full!
また	again
おもしろかった です	it was fun/interesting

Gion festival started more than 1100 years ago when Kyoto was the capital of Japan. It is said that Mt Fuji erupted in 864, which caused extraordinary natural occurrences all over Japan. Kyoto suffered a lot with epidemics then. Gion festival was started to soothe the gods and relieve epidemics.

だい六か

九十一

Talk time
おまつりに行きましたか 🎧

Let's talk about what you did at the festival.

In pairs, practise the model dialogue. Then use the clues 1 and 2 to practise new dialogues.

Person A

おまつりに 行きましたか。

Person B

はい、行きました。

Person A

何を しましたか。

Person B

きれいな ほこを 見ました。

Person A

そう ですか。何を 食べましたか。

Person B

たこやきを 食べました。

Person A

何を 買いましたか。

Person B

おめん 買いました。たのしかった です。

1 イースターショー

大きい うしを 見ました。

ホットドッグ

ショーバッグ

おもしろかった です。

2 ぶんかさい

コンサートに 行きました。

おにぎり

わたあめ

たのしかった です。

| イースターショー | Easter show (the Royal Easter Show) |
| ショーバッグ | show bag |

だい六か

九十二　　　92

Got it?

Receiving presents

もらいます is the verb 'to receive'. To say that you received something like a present or an email, from someone, use the past tense of the verb もらいました with one of the following structures.

[Person]**から** [object]**を** もらいました。   (I) received a [object] **from** [person].

[Person]**に** [object]**を** もらいました。   (I) received a [object] **from** [person].

For example:

わたしは ななこさん **から** 本**を** もらいました。   I received a book **from** Nanako.

わたしは ななこさん**に** 本**を** もらいました。   I received a book **from** Nanako.

We did it together

みんな means 'everyone'. When it is followed by the particle で, it means 'all together'.

You can use みんなで at the beginning of a sentence to talk about something you did as a group.

みんなで カラオケに 行きました。   **Everyone** went to karaoke together.

You can also use みんなで more specifically.

かぞく **みんなで**   **Everyone** in the family

クラス **みんなで**   **Everyone** in the class

サッカーぶ **みんなで** カラオケに 行きました。   **Everyone** in the soccer club went to karaoke together.

Find out more!

仙台に行きました

Michael is staying with りくと's family in Kyoto on homestay. When りくと's family visited 仙台 for their summer holidays, Michael went along.

1. 8月3日に 仙台に 行きました。ホストの お母さんと お父さんと りくとくんと 行きました。

2. りくとくんの おじいさんと おばあさんは 仙台に すんで います。

3. おじいさん、こんにちは！
はじめまして。マイケル です。どうぞ よろしく。

4. きょうは 8月4日 です。おじいさんの たんじょう日 です。77さい です。77さいは たいせつな たんじょう日 です。かぞく みんなで おいわい しました。

5. おたんじょう日 おめでとう ございます。
お父さん、プレゼント です！
みんな、ありがとう。

6. 8月5日に たなばた まつりに 行きました。ゆうめいな おまつり です。お母さんと おばあさんは ゆかたを きました。でも、りくとくんは ゆかたを きません でした。ぼくは はっぴを きました。

Tanabata is a star festival. Special decorations and wishes are hung on bamboo branches. Some areas in Japan celebrate it on 7th of July, but in Sendai, it is in August. *Tanabata* festival originated from China a long time ago. There are other countries that celebrate similar festivals e.g. Korea and Vietnam.

7
やきとりを買います。
やきそばを食べます。
おまつりの やたい です！

8
すごい！
ぼくは はなびが 大好き です。
よる、 はなびを 見ました。

9
はい、おみやげ。
わ〜！ありがとう！
おばあさんに おみやげを もらいました。

10
おじいさん、おばあさん、ありがとう ございました。
8月7日の あさ、しんかんせんの えきに 行きました。

きを つけてね。

11
はい。おばあちゃんも げんきでね！
しんかんせんで 京都（きょうと）に かえりました。

- Some birthdays are more significant than others. In Japan, turning 20, 60, 77, 88 or 99 is very special. Why do you think 77, 88 and 99 years might be considered special?
- What ages are special in your culture?
- Japanese festivals often involve wearing special clothes. What do you think this shows about the festivals?

たいせつ（な）	important; precious
ゆかた	cotton kimono
やきそば	fried noodles
きを つけてね	take care
げんき でね！	Keep well!

だい六か

95 九十五

My vocabulary

Essential たんご

Describing a party
ドレス	dress
きます	wear (clothes)
みんなで	everyone together
おいわい します	celebrate
パーティー	party
もらいます	receive
プレゼント	present; gift
ギフトカード	gift card
よる	night; evening
レストラン	restaurant

Describing how things were
たのしかった です	it was fun
おいしかった です	it was delicious
おもしろかった です	it was fun/interesting
こんで いました	it was crowded

Describing Easter show
イースターショー	Easter show (the Royal Easter Show)
ショーバッグ	show bag

Additional vocabulary
ほこ	portable shrine
やたい	stall

Describing Japanese festivals
はなび	fireworks; sparkles
はっぴ	*happi*; a traditional coat worn at festivals
わたあめ	fairy floss
おめん	mask
ゆかた	*yukata*; cotton kimono
めずらしい	unusual
えんそう します	play; perform (musical instruments)
おとこの 人	man; men
おんなの 人	woman; women
たこやき	octopus dumplings
とうもろこし	corn (on the cob)
やきそば	fried noodles
つめたい	cold
たいせつ (な)	important; precious

Useful expressions
もっと	more
また	again
おなかが いっぱい！	I'm full!
きを つけてね	take care
げんき でね！	Keep well!

Putting it all together 🔑

Birthday celebrations

A group of Japanese students are visiting your school. They are interested in young Australians' lifestyles. Your Japanese teacher asked you to give a speech about how you celebrate birthdays. Write the script for your speech, taking care to answer the following:

- ☐ whose birthday; and when it is
- ☐ who joins the celebration
- ☐ what you do for the celebration
- ☐ also include any special food or clothes for the celebration if applicable.

Local festivals

Create a digital advertisement of a local festival of your choice.

1. Choose a photo or illustration.
2. Write the name of the festival.
3. Include some details: the date, the place, what you can do, see, eat, and buy.

Counting

Counting to 100

1	いち	一
2	に	二
3	さん	三
4	し／よん	四
5	ご	五
6	ろく	六
7	なな／しち	七
8	はち	八
9	く／きゅう	九
10	じゅう	十
11	じゅういち	十一
12	じゅうに	十二
13	じゅうさん	十三
14	じゅうよん	十四
15	じゅうご	十五
16	じゅうろく	十六
17	じゅうなな	十七
18	じゅうはち	十八
19	じゅうきゅう	十九
20	にじゅう	二十

30	さんじゅう	三十
40	よんじゅう	四十
50	ごじゅう	五十
60	ろくじゅう	六十
70	ななじゅう	七十
80	はちじゅう	八十
90	きゅうじゅう	九十
100	ひゃく	百

Conjunctions

そして	and (when used to link sentences)
それから	and then
だから	therefore
でも	but; however

Counting age

1	いっさい	一さい
2	にさい	二さい
3	さんさい	三さい
4	よんさい	四さい
5	ごさい	五さい
6	ろくさい	六さい
7	ななさい	七さい
8	はっさい	八さい
9	きゅうさい	九さい
10	じゅっさい	十さい
11	じゅういっさい	十一さい
12	じゅうにさい	十二さい
13	じゅうさんさい	十三さい
14	じゅうよんさい	十四さい
15	じゅうごさい	十五さい
16	じゅうろくさい	十六さい
17	じゅうななさい	十七さい
18	じゅうはっさい	十八さい
19	じゅうきゅうさい	十九さい
20	にじゅっさい はたち	二十さい

Counting people

1	ひとり	一人
2	ふたり	二人
3	さんにん	三人
4	よにん	四人
5	ごにん	五人
6	ろくにん	六人
7	しちにん ななにん	七人
8	はちにん	八人
9	きゅうにん くにん	九人
10	じゅうにん	十人

Adjectives

い-adjectives

あかるい	cheerful; bright	すごい	amazing
あたまが いい	intelligent	せが たかい	tall (height)
あたらしい	new	せが ひくい	short (height)
いい/よい	good	たのしい	fun; enjoyable
いそがしい	busy	小さい/ちいさい	small
うつくしい	beautiful	つまらない	boring
うるさい	noisy; annoying	つめたい	cold (of liquids)
うれしい	happy	つよい	strong
おいしい	delicious	ながい	long
大きい/おおきい	big	ふるい	old
おもしろい	interesting; funny	みじかい	short
かっこいい	cool; good-looking	むずかしい	hard; difficult
かわいい	cute	めずらしい	rare; unusual
きびしい	strict	やさしい	kind; gentle
こわい	scary		

な-adjectives

一ばん好き(な)/いちばんすき(な)	favourite	大好き(な)/だいすき(な)	really like; love
いや(な)	terrible; disgusting	たいせつ(な)	important; precious
いろいろ(な); いろんな	various	とくい(な)	good at; strong at
きらい(な)	dislike	にがて(な)	weak at; bad at
きれい(な)	pretty; clean	にぎやか(な)	bustling; lively
げんき(な)	fit; healthy	ひま(な)	free (such as time)
しずか(な)	quiet	へん(な)	strange
好き(な)/すき(な)	like; favourite	べんり(な)	convenient
すてき(な)	nice; gorgeous	ゆうめい(な)	famous

Verbs

English	present	past	negative	past negative
meet	あいます	あいました	あいません	あいません でした
hang out; play	あそびます	あそびました	あそびません	あそびません でした
have/take (a shower)	あびます	あびました	あびません	あびません でした
is; exists (things)	あります	ありました	ありません	ありません でした
say	いいます	いいました	いいません	いいません でした
go	行きます	行きました	行きません	行きません でした

九十八

English	present	past	negative	past negative
is; exists (people)	います	いました	いません	いません でした
sing	うたいます	うたいました	うたいません	うたいません でした
sell	うります	うりました	うりません	うりません でした
perform	えんそう します	えんそう しました	えんそう しません	えんそう しません でした
celebrate	おいわい します	おいわい しました	おいわい しません	おいわい しません でした
get up; wake up	おきます	おきました	おきません	おきせまん でした
buy	買います	買いました	買いません	買いません でした
go home; return	かえります	かえりました	かえりません	かえりません でした
write; draw	かきます	かきました	かきません	かきません でした
listen	ききます	ききました	ききません	ききません でした
come; wear (clothes)	きます	きました	きません	きません でした
do; play	します	しました	しません	しません でした
live	すんで います	すんで いました	すんで いません	すんで いません でした
eat	食べます	食べました	食べません	食べません でした
use	つかいます	つかいました	つかいません	つかいません でした
make	つくります	つくりました	つくりません	つくりません でした
build	できます	できました	できません	できません でした
can; able to	できます	できました	できません	できません でした
stay	とまります	とまりました	とまりません	とまりません でした
take	とります	とりました	とりません	とりません でした
learn	ならいます	ならいました	ならいません	ならいません でした
sleep	ねます	ねました	ねません	ねません でした
drink	のみます	のみました	のみません	のみません でした
ride	のります	のりました	のりません	のりません でした
go in; enter	はいります	はいりました	はいりません	はいりません でした
put on; wear (shoes)	はきます	はきました	はきません	はきません でした
talk	はなします	はなしました	はなしません	はなしません でした
play (a musical instrument)	ひきます	ひきました	ひきません	ひきません でした
study	べんきょう します	べんきょう しました	べんきょう しません	べんきょう しません でした
wait	まちます	まちました	まちません	まちません でした
look; see; watch	見ます	見ました	見ません	見ません でした
receive	もらいます	もらいました	もらいません	もらいません でした
read	よみます	よみました	よみません	よみません でした

Particles

は

The particle は is used to mark the topic (or subject) of a sentence. The topic is what the sentence is about. When used as a particle, the character は is pronounced 'wa' instead of 'ha'.

| わたしは まちこ です。 | I am Machiko. |
| わたしは 日本人 です。 | I am Japanese. |

To emphasise a contrast, such as between something big and something small, use は instead of が.

| 目が 大きい です。 | The eyes are big. |
| でも、口は 小さい です。 | However, the mouth is small. |

か

The particle か indicates a question and is similar to the English question mark. It is used at the end of a sentence.

| 何 ですか。 | What is it? |

を

The particle を is placed after the object of a verb. The object of a verb is always a noun (or a pronoun) that explains who or what is affected.

[Object]を [verb]。
| やきゅうを します。 | I play baseball. |

[Object]を ください。
| すしを ください。 | May I have *sushi*, please? |

When talking about presents, use the particle を after the gift, before もらいます.

| ななこさん から 本を もらいました。 | I received a book from Nanako. |

と

The particle と means 'and'. It is used between items in a list.

[Object 1]と [object 2]を ください。
| さしみと てんぷらを ください。 | May I have *sashimi* and *tempura*, please? |

The particle と can also be used to mean 'with' someone.

| ともだちと おひるごはんを 食べます。 | I eat lunch with friends. |

の

The particle の works like the combination of an apostrophe and 's' does in English; it shows possession or ownership.

[Person]の [object]
| ゆうなさんの でんわ ばんごうは？ | What is Yuuna's telephone number? |

が

When saying that you (or another person) like something, you use が after the thing you like, followed by 好きです.

[Topic]は [object]が 好き です。
| わたしは おんがくが 好き です。 | I like music. |

The particle が is also used when describing people.

[Person]は [body part]が [adjective] です。
pi ka chu u
| ピカチュウは 目が 大きい です。 | Pikachu has big eyes. |

に

The particle に has many different uses. It can mean 'to', 'at', 'on', 'in' or 'for'. Use に:

- after the place you are going to

| まちに 行きます。 | (I am) going to the city. |

- after places to mean 'in'

| おふろに はいります。 | I take a bath. |
| とうきょうに すんで います。 | I live in Tokyo. |

- after the day you are talking about to say what you do on a certain day

| 日よう日に 日本語を べんきょう します。 | (I) study Japanese on Sundays. |

百

100

- with various time expressions to mean 'at', 'on' or 'in'

何時に	at what time
7時半に	at 7:30
月よう日に	on Monday
一月三日に	on 3 January
三月に	in March

- after meals to mean 'for'

| あさごはんに | for breakfast |
| あさごはんに ごはんを 食べます。 | I eat rice for breakfast. |

- before some verbs that use the particle に instead of を

_{mi k ki i}
| ミッキーに あいました。 | I met Mickey (Mouse). |

- when taking a ride

_{su pe e su ma u n te n}
| スペースマウンテンに のりました。 | I rode on Space Mountain |

- when talking about receiving something, it is used after the person who gave it to you.

| ななこさんに 本を もらいました。 | (I) received a book from Nanako. |

Sometimes, に can be used more than once in a sentence.

_{とうきょう}
| 9月20日に 東京に 行きます。 | (We are) going to Tokyo on 20 September. |

も

The particle も means 'and', 'also' or 'too'.

おもしろい みせも あります。	There are also interesting shops.
目も 耳も 小さい です。	His eyes and his ears are small.
そして 口も 小さい です。	And his mouth is small too.

で

The particle で is used after the method of transport to mean 'by'.

| 何で 学校に 行きますか。 | How do you go to school? |
| バスで 学校に 行きます。 | I go to school by bus. |

The particle で is also used after the place where you do an action to mean 'at' or 'in'.

_{sa k ka a}
| よく こうえんで サッカーを します。 | I often play soccer in the park. |

The particle で is also used after みんな to mean 'all together'.

_{ka ra o ke}
| みんなで カラオケに 行きました。 | Everyone went to *karaoke* together. |

The particle で shows reason or cause.

_{ひろしま}
| 広島は おこのみやきで ゆうめい です。 | Hiroshima is famous for *Okonomiyaki*. |

から *and* まで

In Japanese, 'from' is から and 'until' is まで. You can use them together or separately when talking about times and places.

ひるやすみは 12時半 から 1時20分 まで です。	Lunch is from 12.30 until 1.20.
えき から 学校 まで バスで 行きます。	From the station to the school, I go by bus.
はるは 五月 まで です。	Spring is until May.

_{ba su}

When talking about receiving something, the particle から is used after the person who gave it to you.

| ななこさん から 本を もらいました。 | (I) received a book from Nanako. |

や

The particle や is used instead of と to mean 'and' in a list of things where not everything is listed. It gives the meaning of 'etc.' or 'and so on'.

_{ho t to do g gu}
| ホットドッグと おにぎりを うります。 | We sell hotdogs and rice balls. |
_{ho t to do g gu}
| ホットドッグや おにぎりを うります。 | We sell hotdogs and rice balls, among other things. |

Grammar summary

Here is a summary of what you have learnt in *iiTomo 1* and *iiTomo 2*.

All about me

（わたし／ぼく）は [name] です。
　I am [name].
（わたしは）鈴木かずこ or 鈴木和子 です。
　I am Kazuko Suzuki. (My name is Kazuko Suzuki.)
ぼくの なまえは 鈴木けん or 鈴木健 です。
　My name is Ken Suzuki.
でんわ ばんごうは?
　What is your telephone number?
わたしの でんわ ばんごうは [number] です。
　My telephone number is [number].
[Name] は 何さい ですか。
　How old is [name]?
何さい ですか。
　How old (are you)?
（わたし／ぼくは [number]さい です。
　I am [number] years old.
（わたし／ぼく）は 十三さい です。
　I am thirteen years old.
しゅみは 何 ですか。
　What is your hobby?
（しゅみは）スポーツ です。
　(My hobby) is sport.
何年生 ですか。
　What year are you in?
中学2年生 です。
　I am a second year junior high school student.
スキーが できますか。
　Can you do skiing?
はい、できます。
　Yes, I can do it.
いいえ、できません。
　No, I can't do it.

Family

かぞくは 何人 ですか。
　How many people are in your family?
かぞくは [number]人 です。
　There are [number] people in my family.
（かぞくは）四人 です。
　There are four people (in my family).

[Person]と [person]と わたし です。
　My family is [person] and [person] and me.
父と 母と あねと わたし です。
　My family is my dad, my mum, my elder sister and me.
[Family term]の [name] です。
　This is my [family term], [name].
母の さちこ です。
　This is my mother, Sachiko.
えりこさんの かぞくは 三人 です。お父さんと お母さんと えりこさん です。
　There are three people in Eriko's family. Her father, mother, and Eriko.
[Family member – for others]が いますか。
　Do you have a(n) [family member]?
おにいさんが いますか。
　Do you have an elder brother?
はい、[family member – for your own] がいます。
　Yes, I have a(n) [family member].
はい、あにが います。
　Yes, I have an elder brother.
いいえ、いません。
　No, I do not.

Friends

[Person]は [body part]が [adjective]です。
　ともだちは 目が 大きい です。
　My friend has big eyes.
目も 口も 小さい です。
　Her eyes and her mouth are both small.
目が 大きい です。でも、口は 小さい です。
　Her eyes are big. However, her mouth is small.
[Name]さん（くん）は [adjective] です。
広一くんは おもしろい です。
　Kōichi is funny.
ジョンくんは つよくて かっこいい です。
　John is strong and cool.
まさこさんは へんで おもしろい です。
　Masako is strange and interesting.
みんなで カラオケに 行きました。
　Everyone went to *karaoke* together.

Where I live

どこに すんで いますか。
Where do you live?

^{ひろしま}
広島に すんで います。
I live in Hiroshima.

^{ひろしま}
広島は おこのみやきで ゆうめい です。
Hiroshima is famous for *Okonomiyaki*.

^{きょうと}
京都は どんな まち ですか。
What kind of town is Kyoto?

^{きょうと}
京都は ふるい まち です。
Kyoto is an old town.

^{きょうと}
京都は ゆうめいな まち です。
Kyoto is a famous town.

^{きょうと}
京都は ゆうめい です。
Kyoto is famous.

[Item]が ありますか。
Is there [item]?
にわが ありますか。
Is there a garden?

[Adjective] [item(s)]が あります。
There are [adjective] [item(s)].
うつくしい にわが あります。
There are beautiful gardens.
ゆうめいな にわが あります。
There are famous gardens.

[Adjective] [item(s)]も あります。
There are also [adjective] [item(s)].
おもしろい みせも あります。
There are also interesting shops.

Ordering food

何を たべますか。
What would you eat?

ぼくは さかなは あんまり。だから、やきとりを たべます。
I am not keen on fish and therefore I will eat *yakitori*.

ごちゅうもんは?
Your order is..?

すしを ください。
May I have sushi, please?

すしと てんぷらを おねがいします。
May I have sushi and tempura?

Likes and dislikes

[Person]は [item]が 好き です。
[Person] likes [item].
わたしは おんがくが 好き です。
I like music.

^{supōtsu}
スポーツが 好き ですか。
Do you like sport?
はい、好き です。　　　Yes, I like it.
はい、大好き です。　　Yes, I love it.
いいえ、あんまり...。　No, not really.

^{supōtsu}
どんな スポーツが 好き ですか。
What kind of sport do you like?
やきゅうが 好き です。
I like baseball.

[Item]は 好き じゃない です。
I do not like [item].
やきゅうは 好き じゃない です。
I do not like baseball.

好きな かもくは 何 ですか。
What is a subject that you like?
おんがく です。
Music.
にがてな かもくは かていか です。
A subject that I am weak at is home economics.

Going places

どこに 行きますか。
Where do you go?

[Place]に 行きます
I go to [place].
まちに 行きます。
I go to the city.

[Place]に 行きません。
I do not go to [place].
まちに 行きません。
I do not go to the city.

[Transport mode]で [place]に 行きます。
I go to [place] by [transport mode].

^{なん}
何で 学校に 行きますか。
How do you go to school?
^{basu}
バスで 学校に 行きます。
I go to school by bus.

[Place 1]から [place 2]まで [transport mode]で 行きます。
I go from [Place 1] to [place 2] by [transport mode].
^{basu}
えき から 学校 まで バスで 行きます。
I go by bus from the station to school.

School

1時かんめは 何 ですか。
What is the first period?

The [number of period] is [subject].
1時かんめは 日本語 です。
The first period is Japanese.

はい、1時かんめは 日本語 です。
Yes, first period is Japanese.

いいえ、1時かんめは 日本語 じゃない です。
No, first period is not Japanese.

2時かんめは 何時 から ですか。
From what time is second period?
10時 から です。
It is from 10 o'clock.

日本語は 何時かんめ ですか。
What period is Japanese?

[Subject]は [number of period] です。
日本語は 1時かんめ です。
The first period is Japanese.

1時かんめは 日本語 ですか。
Is first period Japanese?

学校は 何時 から 何時 まで ですか。
School is from what time to what time?
学校は 9時 から 3時 まで です。
School is from 9 o'clock until 3 o'clock.

休みに 学校の 本を よみません でした。
I did not read school books in the holidays.

先生に あいました。
I met my teacher.

Daily routines

何時に おきますか。
What time do you get up?

何時に おきましたか。
What time did you get up?

何時に ねますか。
What time do you go to bed?

何時に ねましたか。
What time did you go to bed?

[Time]に [place]に 行きました。
I went to [place] at [time].
7時半に 学校に 行きました。
I went to school at 7.30.

ひるごはんに 何を 食べますか。
What do you eat for lunch?

[Meal]に [food]を 食べます。
I eat [food] for [meal].
ひるごはんに ごはんを 食べます。
I eat rice for lunch.

にくと ごはんを 食べます。
I eat meat and rice.

ともだちと きゅうしょくを 食べます。
I eat school lunch with friends.

[Place]で [activity]を [verb]。
よく こうえんで サッカーを します。
sa k ka a
I often play soccer in the park.

まい日 [activity]を [verb]か。
Do you do [activity] every day?
まい日 ぶかつを しますか。
Do you do club activities every day?

はい、まい日 ぶかつを します。
Yes, I do club activities every day.
いいえ、しません。
No, I do not.

Telling the time

いま、何時 ですか。
What time is it now?

いま、[time] です。
It is now [time].
いま、3時半 です。
It is now 3.30.

Days of the week

日よう日に 何を しますか。
What do you do on Sundays?

[Day]に [activity]を [verb]。
日よう日に ゲームを します。
ge e mu
I play games on Sundays.

何よう日に テニスを しますか。
te ni su
Which day do you play tennis?

月よう日に テニスを します。
te ni su
I play tennis on Mondays.

[Day]に 何をしますか。
> What do you do on [day]?

土よう日に 何を しますか。
> What do you do on Saturdays?

土よう日に テニス(te ni su)を しますか。
> Do you play tennis on Saturdays?

いいえ、しません。
> No, I don't.

いいえ、テニス(te ni su)をしません。やきゅうをします。
> No, I do not play tennis. I play baseball.

[Day] に どこに 行きますか。
> Where do you go on [day]?

土よう日に どこに 行きますか。
> Where do you go on Saturdays?

Dates, months and seasons

[Season]は [month]から [month]です。
> [Season] is from [month] to [month].

はるは 3月 から 5月 まで です。
> Spring is from March until May.

[Event]は いつ ですか。
> When is the [event]?

はるの えんそくは いつ ですか。
> When is the spring excursion?

[Event]は [date] です。
> The spring excursion is on 25 May.

はるの えんそくは 5月25日 です。
> The spring excursion is on 25 May.

いつ、[event]が ありますか。
> When is the [event]?

いつ、えんそくが ありますか。
> When is the excursion?

[Date]に [event]が あります。
> On [date] there is [event].

5月25日に えんそくが あります。
> On 25 May there is an excursion.

[Date]に [place]に 行きます。
> I am going to [place] on [date].

9月20日に 東京(とうきょう)に 行きます。
> I am going to Tokyo on 20 September.

How often?

よくけいたいを つかいます。
> I often use a mobile phone.

ときどき けいたいを つかいます。
> I sometimes use a mobile phone.

あまり けいたいを つかいません。
> I do not use a mobile phone very often.

ぜんぜん けいたいを つかいません。
> I do not use a mobile phone at all.

Gifts

[Person]から [item]を もらいました。
> I received a [item] from [person].

わたしは ななこさん から 本を もらいました。
> I received a book from Nanako.

[Person]に [item]を もらいました。
> I received a [item] from [person].

わたしは ななこさんに 本を もらいました。
> I received a book from Nanako.

Other

ホットドッグ(ho t todo g gu)と おにぎりを うります。
> We sell hotdogs and rice balls.

ホットドッグ(ho t todo g gu)や おにぎりを うります。
> We sell hotdogs and rice balls, among other things.

コートを よく きますか。
> Do you often wear a coat?

ジーンズを よく はきますか。
> Do you often wear a pair of jeans?

みひろさんは 何を きて いますか。
> What is Mihiro wearing?

みひろさんは ブラウスを きて います。
> Mihiro is wearing a blouse.

そして、スカートを はいて います。
> And she is wearing a skirt.

それから、ネクタイを して います。
> Then she also has got a tie on.

Japanese–English

あ・ア

ああ	oh
アーケード　*aakeedo*	arcade
アイス スケート　*aisu sukeeto*	ice skating
あいます	meet
あかるい	cheerful; bright
あき	autumn
アクセス　*akusesu*	access
あさ	morning
あさごはん	breakfast
あさって	day after tomorrow
あし	foot; leg
あした	tomorrow
あそびます	hang out; play
あたま	head
あたらしい	new
あに	my elder brother
アニメ　*anime*	anime; animation
アニメグッズ　*animeguzzu*	animation goods
あね	my elder sister
あびます	have/take (*a shower*)
あまり	not much
あまり ～ません	rarely; not often
ありがとう	thank you (*casual*)
ありがとう ございました	thank you (*polite*)
あります	is; exists (*for non-living things*)
あるいて	walking; on foot
アルバム　*arubamu*	album
アンケート　*ankeeto*	questionnaire
あんまり; あまり	not much

い・イ

いい	good
いいえ	no
イースターショー　*iisutaashoo*	Easter show
いいですね	sounds good
いいですか	is it OK?
いいます	say
伊賀　*iga*	Iga
行きます　*ikimasu*	go
いそがしい	busy
いただきます	an expression of thanks said before eating
一　*ichi*	one
一月　*ichigatsu*	January
一学き　*ichigakki*	Term One
一ばん好き(な)　*ichibansuki (na)*	favourite
いつ	when
いっしょに	together
いつも	always
イベント　*ibento*	event
いま	now
います	is; exists (*for living things*)
いもうと	my younger sister
いもうとさん	younger sister
いやだ	yuck; terrible
いらっしゃいませ	welcome (*to a shop or restaurant*)
いりぐち	entrance
いろいろ(な)	various
インタビュー　*intabyuu*	interview

う・ウ

うし	cow
うた	song
うたいます	sing
うち	house
うちにいます	stay at home
うつくしい	beautiful
うみ	sea; ocean
うります	sell
うれしい	happy
うわばき	indoor shoes; slippers
うんどうぶ	sports clubs

え・エ

え	drawing; picture
エアロビクス　*earobikusu*	aerobics
えいが	movie
えいかいわ	English conversation
えい語　*eigo*	English
えき	station
えにっき	picture diary
eメール　*iimeeru*	email
円　*en*	yen
えんげき	theatre
えんそう します	play; perform
えんそく	excursion

お・オ

おいしい	delicious
おいわい します	celebrate
おいしかった です	it was delicious
大きい　*ōkii*	big
大阪じょう　*oosaka jō*	Osaka castle
オーストラリア　*ōsutoraria*	Australia
オーストラリア人　*ōsutorariajin*	Australian person
お母さま　*okaasama*	mother (*polite*)
お母さん　*okaasan*	mother
お母ちゃん　*okaachan*	mum
(お)かし	sweets; lollies
おきます	get up; wake up
(お)こづかい	pocket money
おじいさん	grandfather
(お)しろ	castle
(お)たんじょう日　*(o) tanjōbi*	birthday
おたんじょう日おめでとう *o tanjōbi omedeto*	happy birthday (*casual*)
おたんじょう日おめでとう ございます *o tanjōbi omedeto gozaimasu*	happy birthday (*polite*)
オッケー　*okkee*	OK
(お)てら	temple
お父さん　*otōsan*	father
おとうと	my younger brother
おとうとさん	younger brother
男の子　*otokonoko*	boy; boys
男の人　*otokonohito*	man; men
おどろいた	was/were surprised
(お)ちゃ	green tea
おなか	stomach
おなかが いっぱい	I'm full
おにいさん	elder brother
おにぎり	rice ball

百六　　106

おねえさん	elder sister
おばあさん	grandmother
（お）はし	chopsticks
おはよう	good morning (*casual*)
おはよう ございます	good morning (*polite*)
（お）ひるごはん	lunch
（お）ふろ	bath
（お）べんとう	lunch box; packed lunch
（お）まつり	festival
（お）みやげ	souvenir
おめでとう	congratulations (*casual*)
おめでとう ございます	congratulations (*polite*)
おめん	mask
おもしろい	interesting; funny
おもしろかった です	it was interesting; funny
おりがみ	origami
おんがく	music
女の子　onnanoko	girl; girls
女の人　onnanohito	woman; women
オンラインゲーム　onrain geemu	online game

か・カ

カーディガン　kaadigan	cardigan
買います　kaimasu	buy
買いもの　kaimono	shopping
かえります	go home; return
かお	face
か学　kagaku	science
かきます	write; draw
学生　gakusei	student
（お）かし	sweets; lollies
かぞく	family
かたな	sword
かっこいい	cool; good-looking
学校　gakkō	school
かていか	home economics
かぶっています	is wearing (for head)
かぶります	to wear (for head)
かみ（のけ）	hair
かもく	school subject
火よう日　kayōbi	Tuesday
から	from
カラオケ　karaoke	*karaoke*
からて	*karate*
カレンダー　karendaa	calendar
川　kawa	river
かわいい	cute
かわいそう	poor thing
がんばって ください	please do your best
がんばれ！	hang in there!

き・キ

ぎおん まつり	Gion festival
ききます	listen
ぎじゅつ	technology
ギター　gitaa	guitar
きって	(postage) stamp
きています	is wearing (for upper or whole body)
きてください	please come
ギフトカード　gifutokaado	gift card
きびしい	strict
きました	came
きます	come; wear (*clothes*)
キャラクター　kyarakutaa	character
きゅうしょく	school lunch
キュート（な）　kyuuto (na)	cute
ぎゅうにゅう	milk
きょう	today
きょうしつ	classroom

きょうだい	siblings
きょ年　kyonen	last year
キラキラ　kirakira	twinkle twinkel
きれい（な）	pretty; clean
きを つけてね	take care
金よう日　kinyōbi	Friday

く・ク

九月　kugatsu	September
ください	please
くだもの	fruit
口　kuchi	mouth
グッズ　guzzu	goods; merchandise
熊本県　kumamoto ken	Kumamoto prefecture
くもり	cloudy
グラウンド　guraundo	school grounds
クラシック　kurashikku	classic
クラス　kurasu	class
クリケット　kuriketto	cricket
グループ　guruupu	group
くるま	car
～くん	Mr (*for young men and boys*)

け・ケ

けいたい でんわ	mobile phone
ケーキ　keeki	cake
ケータイ　keetai	mobile phone (*slang*)
ゲーム　geemu	game
月よう日　getsuyōbi	Monday
げんき（な）	fit; healthy
げんきでね！	keep well!
けんどう	*kendo*; Japanese fencing

こ・コ

こうえん	park
高校　kōkō	senior high school
高校生	senior high school student
コート　kooto	coat
コーヒー　kōhii	coffee
コーラ　kōra	cola
五月　gogatsu	May
こく語　kokugo	national language; Japanese
ここ	here; this place
コスプレ　kosupure	cosplay; costume play
ことば	word
こども	child
このひと	this person
ごはん人　hito	rice
コメント　komento	comment
こら	hey
コロッケ　korokke	croquette
こわい	scary
コンサート　konsaato	concert
こんでいました	it was crowded
こんど	this time
コンピューター　konpyuutaa	computer
コンピューター ゲーム　konpyuutaa geemu	computer game

さ・サ

サービス　saabisu	service
～さい	—— years old
さいこう	best
サッカー　sakkaa	soccer
ざっし	magazine
サフランライス　safuran raisu	saffron rice
さむらい	*samurai*

Vocabulary

三月 sangatsu	March
三学き sangakki	Term Three
サンキュー sankyuu	Thank you
サンダル sandaru	sandals
さんぽ	stroll; walk

し・シ

〜時 ji	... o'clock
ジーンズ jiinzu	jeans
しあい	games; match
Jポップ jee poppu	J-pop
しか	deer
四月 shigatsu	April
時かん jikan	time; hour
〜時かんめ jikanme	period ——
時かんわり jikanwari	timetable
しけん	exam
じこしょうかい	self-introduction
しずか（な）	quiet
七月 shichigatsu	July
じっけん	experiment
しっぽ	tail
じてんしゃ	bicycle
します	do; wear (small items)
じゃ	then; well then
じゃあ（ね）	well then; see you
しゃかい	social sciences
じゃがいも	potato
ジャケット jaketto	jacket
しゃしん	photo
ジャズ jazu	Jazz
〜じゃない です	is not
ジャパニメ japanime	Japanese animation
シャワー shawaa	shower
十一月 juuichigatsu	November
しゅう学りょこう shuugakuryoko	school trip
十月 juugatsu	October
じゅうどう	judo
十二月 juunigatsu	December
しゅうまつ	weekend
じゅく	cram school
しゅくだい	homework
しゅみ	hobby
しゅりけん	throwing star
小学校 shōgakkō	primary school
小学生 shōgakusei	primary school student
じょうずに	well; skillfully
ショーバッグ shoobaggu	show bag
しょどう	calligraphy
（お）しろ	castle
しんかんせん	*shinkansen*; bullet train
じんじゃ	shrine

す・ス

すいえい	swimming
すいえいたいかい	swimming carnival
水よう日 suiyōbi	Wednesday
スープ suupu	soup
すう学 suugaku	mathematics
スカート sukaato	skirt
スキー skii	ski
好き（な） suki (na)	like; favourite
好きじゃない suki janai	dislike
好き です suki desu	like
すきやき	a Japanese meal
スクールバス sukuurubasu	school bus
スクラップブック sukurappubukku	scrapbook
すごい	great; amazing
すてき（な）	nice; gorgeous
スポーツ supōtsu	sports

すみません	excuse me
すんでいます	live; is living

せ・ゼ

せ	body height
セーター seetaa	jumper
せいふく	uniform
せかい中 sekai juu	worldwide
せが高い se ga takai	tall (height)
せがひくい	short (height)
せつめいする	explain
ゼロ zero	zero
先しゅう senshuu	last week
先生 sensei	teacher
ぜんぜん 〜ません	never; not at all

そ・ソ

そうじ	cleaning
そして	and (*when used to link sentences*)
ソックス sokkusu	socks
そ父 sofu	my grandfather
そ母 sobo	my grandmother
それから	and then
ソニー sonii	Sony
それに	furthermore

た・タ

たいいく	PE; physical education
たいいくさい	sports festival
大学 daigaku	university
大好き（な） daisuki (na)	really like; love
たいせつ（な）	important; precious
たいそう	gymnastics
たいてい	usually; generally
大ぶつ daibutsu	large statue of Buddha
ダウンロード daunrōdo	download
（せが）高い (se ga) takai	tall (height)
だから	therefore
たくさん	lots; many
タクシー takushii	taxi
たこやき	octopus dumplings
たなばたまつり	*Tanabata* festival
たのしい	fun; enjoyable
たのしかった です	it was fun
食べてください tabete kudasai	please eat
食べます tabemasu	eat
食べもの tabemono	food
だれ	who
（お）たんじょう日 (o) tanjōbi	birthday
ダンス dansu	dance
だんらく	paragraph

ち・チ

小さい chiisai	small
ちがう	different
父 chichi	my father
（お）ちゃ	green tea
チャット chatto	chat
〜ちゃん	Miss; Master
中学校 chuugakkō	junior high school
中学生 chuugakusei	junior high school student
チョコバナナ choko banana	chocolate-coated banana
ちょっと	little bit; umm
ちょっと いい ですか	may I interrupt you?
ちり	geography
チリコンカン	chilli con carne

百八

つ・ツ

一日　tsuitachi	first day of the month
つかいます	use
月　tsuki	moon
つぎ	next
つくります	make
つけもの	pickles
つまらない	boring
つめたい	cold (*of liquids*)
つよい	strong
つり	fishing

て・テ

手　te	hand
デートを します　deeto o shimasu	go on a date
T－シャツ　tii shatsu	T-shirt
できました	was built
(が) できます	can; able to
(が) できません	can't (do/play)
でした	was
です	(it) is; (I) am
テスト　tesuto	test
ですね	isn't it?
テニス　tenisu	tennis
では	then
デパート　depaato	department store
でも	but
(お) てら	temple
テレビ　terebi	television
でんしゃ	train
テント　tento	tent

と・ト

と	and
どうして	why
どうしよう	what should I do?
どうぞ	here you are
どうぞ よろしく	nice to see/meet you (*casual*); please take good care of me
どうぞ よろしく おねがい します	nice to see you (*polite*); please take good care of me
トースト　tosuto	toast
どう でしたか	how was it?
どうとく	ethics
十日　tōka	tenth day of the month
時　toki	time; when
とうもろこし	corn
ときどき	sometimes
ドキドキ　dokidoki	an anomatopoeic expression – beating heart
とくい (な)	good at; strong at
どくしょ	reading (*as a hobby*)
とけい	clock; watch
どこ	where
ところ	place
どっち	which one of the two (*casual form*)
とても	very
どの人　donohito	which person
とまります	stay
ともだち	friend
土よう日　doyōbi	Saturday
トヨタ　toyota	Toyota
どらやき	pancake with sweet red bean
とります	take
どれ	which one (of the three or more)
ドレス　doresu	dress
どんな	what kind of; what sort of

な・ナ

ながい	long
なぜ	why
なつ	summer
なつ休み　natsuyasumi	summer holiday
七日　nanoka	seventh day of the month
ナビサービス　nabisaabisu	navigator service
奈良　nara	Nara
ならいごと	extra curricular activities
ならいます	learn
何　nan; nani	what
何月　nangatsu	what month
何時　nanji	what time
何時から　nanji kara	from what time
何時まで　nanji made	until what time
何時かんめ　nanjikanme	what period
何で　nande	by what means; how
何日　nannichi	what day
何人　nannin	how many people
何年生　nannensei	what grade; what year level
何よう日　nanyōbi	what day (*of the week*)

に・ニ

二　ni	two
二月　nigatsu	February
二学き　nigakki	Term Two
にがて (な)	weak at; bad at
にぎやか (な)	bustling; lively
にく	meat
日よう日　nichiyōbi	Sunday
にている	similar
日本　nihon	Japan
日本語　nihongo	Japanese language
日本人　nihonjin	Japanese person
日本中　nihon juu	all over Japan
にゅう学しき　nyuugakushiki	school entrance ceremony
にわ	garden
にんきが あります	popular
にんじゃ	*ninja*
にんじゃしき	*ninja* house
にんじん	carrot

ぬ・ヌ

ね・ネ

ねえ	hey
ねます	sleep
ネクタイ　nekutai	neck tie
ネットボール　netto booru	netball
年　nen	year
～年生　nensei	Year level

の・ノ

のみます	drink
のります	ride

は・ハ

パーカー　paakaa	hoodie
パーティー　paatii	party
はい	yes
バイバイ　baibai	bye-bye; goodbye (*casual*)
はいります	go in; enter
はきます	to wear (for lower part of body)
(お) はし	chopsticks
バス　basu	bus
バスケットボール　basukettobōru	basketball
はたち	twenty years old

Vocabulary

八 hachi		eight
八月 hachigatsu		August
二十日 hatsuka		twentieth day of the month
はっぴ		*happi* coat
はな		nose
はなします		talk
はなび		fireworks
母 haha		my mother
はやく		early; fast; quickly
原宿 harajuku		Harajuku, city in Tokyo
はる		spring
はる休み haruyasumi		spring holiday
はるまき		spring roll
はれ		fine; sunny
バレエ baree		ballet
半 han		half
ばんごはん		dinner
パンツ pantsu		pants

ひ・ヒ

日 hi	sun
ビーチ biichi	beach
ピアノ piano	piano
ひきます	play (*a musical instrument*)
(せが)ひくい (se ga hikui)	short (height)
ひこうき	aeroplane
びじゅつ	art
ひだり	left
人 hito	person
一人 hitori	one person
一人っこ hitorikko	only child
ひま(な)	free (*such as time*)
百 hyaku	one hundred
100円ショップ hyaku en shoppu	100-yen shop
(お)ひるごはん	lunch
ひる休み hiruyasumi	lunch break

ふ・フ

～ぶ	[activity] club
ファン fan	fan
ブーツ buutsu	boots
プール puuru	pool
フォーラム fōramu	forum
ぶかつ	club activity (at school)
ふく	clothes
二人 futari	two people
二日 futsuka	second day of the month
フットボール futto booru	football
ふゆ	winter
ふゆ休み fuyuyasumi	winter holiday
ブラウス burausu	blouse
ふるい	old
プレゼント purezento	present; gift
(お)ふろ	bath
ブログ burogu	blog
プロフィール purofiiru	profile
分 fun; pun; bun	minute
ぶんかさい	school culture festival
ぶんぽう	grammar

へ・ヘ

ペア pea	pair
へいわこうえん	Peace Park
ベスト besuto	vest
へや	room
ベルト beruto	belt
へん(な)	strange
べんきょう します	study
(お)べんとう	lunch box; packed lunch
べんり(な)	convenient

ほ・ホ

ぼうし	hat
ホームルーム hōmuruumu	homeroom
ほか	other
ぼく	I; me; myself (*boy*)
ぼくたち	we (*for boys*)
ぼくの	my (*for boys*)
ほこ	portable shrine
ポスター posutaa	poster
ホスト ファミリー hosuto famirii	host family
ほたる	firefly
ホットドッグ hotto doggu	hotdog
本 hon	book
ほんとう(に)	true; really

ま・マ

まい年 maitoshi	every year
まい日 mainichi	every day
～ました	did
マスコット masukotto	mascot
～ませんでした	did not do
まだ	not yet
また	again
また あした	see you tomorrow
まち	town; city
(お)まつり	festival
まで	until
マフラー mafuraa	scarf
まる	full stop; circle
まんが	manga; comic book
まんがきっさ	manga café
まんがか	cartoonist

み・ミ

みぎ	right
みじかい	short
水 mizu	water
みせ	shop
みそ	miso
三日 mikka	third day of the month
見て！ mite	look!
見てください mite kudasai	please watch
みなさん	everyone
見ます mimasu	look; see; watch
耳 mimi	ear
ミュージカル myuujikaru	musical
みんな	everyone
みんなで	everyone together

む・ム

六日 muika	sixth day of the month
むずかしい	hard; difficult

め・メ

目 me	eye
めずらしい	rare; unusual
メンバー menbaa	member

も・モ

も	also; too
もう いちど	once again; one more time
もっと	more
もらいます	receive
木よう日 mokuyōbi	Thursday

や・ヤ

やきそば		fried noodles
やきもの		pottery
やきゅう		baseball
やさしい		nice; gentle; kind
やった		yippee
山	yama	mountain
休み	yasumi	holiday
やたい		stall

ゆ・ユ

ゆうめい（な）		famous
ゆかた		cotton kimono
ゆっくり		slowly
ユニクロ	yunikuro	Uniqlo

よ・ヨ

よい		good
八日	yōka	eighth day of the month
よかった		was good
よく		often
よく できました		well done
四日	yokka	fourth day of the month
よみます		read
よる		night; evening
よろい		armour

ら・ラ

ライス		rice

り・リ

りか		science
りょうしん		my parents
りょうり		cooking

る・ル

れ・レ

れい		zero
れきし		history
レストラン	resutoran	restaurant
れつ		row
レッスン	ressun	lesson
れんしゅう		practice

ろ・ロ

六	roku	six
六月	rokugatsu	June
ロック	rokku	rock 'n' roll
ロボット	robotto	robot

わ・ワ

わあ		wow
わかりました		understood
わかります		understand
わたあめ		fairy floss
わたし		I; me; myself
わたしたち		we (*for girls*)
わたしの		my
わふう		Japanese-style
ワンワン	wan wan	woof woof (dog bark)

を・ヲ

〜を ください		may I have [item]?

ん・ン

English–Japanese

A

able to	できます
access	アクセス　akusesu
aerobics	エアロビクス　earobikusu
aeroplane	ひこうき
again	また
album	アルバム　arubamu
all over Japan	日本中　nihon juu
also	も
always	いつも
amazing	すごい
and	そして (*when used to link sentences*); と (*between words*)
and then	それから
animation; anime	アニメ　anime
animation goods	アニメグッズ　animeguzzu
April	四月　shigatsu
arcade	アーケード　aakeedo
armour	よろい
art	びじゅつ
attractive	すてき（な）
August	八月　hachigatsu
Australia	オーストラリア　ōsutoraria
Australian person	オーストラリア人　ōsutorariajin
autumn	あき

B

bad at	にがて（な）
ballet	バレエ　baree
baseball	やきゅう
basketball	バスケットボール　basukettobōru
bath	（お）ふろ
beach	ビーチ　biichi
bean paste	みそ　miso
beautiful	うつくしい
best	さいこう
belt	ベルト　beruto
bicycle	じてんしゃ
big	大きい　ōkii
birthday	（お）たんじょう日　(o) tanjōbi
blog	ブログ　burogu
blouse	ブラウス　burausu
book	本　hon
boots	ブーツ　buutsu
boring	つまらない
boxing	ボクシング　bokushingu
boy; boys	男の子　otokonoko
breakfast	あさごはん
bright	あかるい
brother (elder)	おにいさん；あに
brother (younger)	おとうとさん；おとうと

Vocabulary

Buddha (large statue of Buddha)	大ぶつ	daibutsu
(is/was) built	できました	
bullet train	しんかんせん	
bus	バス	basu
bustling	にぎやか（な）	
busy	いそがしい	
but	でも	
buy	買います	kaimasu
by what means	何で	nande
bye-bye	バイバイ	baibai

C

cake	ケーキ	keeki
calendar	カレンダー	karendaa
calligraphy	しょどう	
can	できます	
car	くるま	
castle	（お）しろ	
celebrate	おいわい します	
character	キャラクター	kyarakutaa
chat	チャット	chatto
cheerful	あかるい	
child	こども	
chilli con carne	チリコンカン	chirikonkan
chocolate-coated banana	チョコバナナ	choko banana
chopsticks	（お）はし	
circle	まる	
city	まち	
class	クラス	kurasu
classic	クラシック	kurashikku
classroom	きょうしつ	
clean	きれい（な）	
cleaning	そうじ	
clock	とけい	
cloudy	くもり	
—— club	〜ぶ	
club activity (at school)	ぶかつ；ぶかつどう	
coat	コート	kōto
coffee	コーヒー	kōhii
cola	コーラ	kōra
cold (of liquids)	つめたい	
come	きます	
comic book	まんが	
comment	コメント	komento
computer	コンピューター	konpyuutaa
computer game	コンピューター ゲーム	konpyuutaa geemu
concert	コンサート	konsaato
congratulations	おめでとう (casual)；おめでとう ございます (polite)	
convenient	べんり（な）	
cooking	りょうり	
cool	かっこいい	
corn	とうもろこし	
cosplay; costume play	コスプレ	kosupure
cotton kimono	ゆかた	
cow	うし	
cram school	じゅく	
cricket	クリケット	kuriketto
croquette	コロッケ	korokke
crowded (was)	こんでいました	
culture club	ぶんかぶ	
cute	かわいい；キュート（な）	kyuuto (na)

D

dance	ダンス	dansu
date (go on a)	デートを します	deetoo shimasu
day after tomorrow	あさって	
December	十二月	juunigatsu
deer	しか	
delicious	おいしい	
department store	デパート	depaato
did	〜ました	
did not	〜ませんでした	
different	ちがう	
difficult	むずかしい	
dinner	ばんごはん	
dislike	好き じゃない　suki janai；きらい（な）	
do	します	
download	ダウンロード	daunrōdo
draw	かきます	
drawing	え	
dress	ドレス	doresu
drink	のみます	

E

ear	耳	mimi
early	はやく	
Easter show	イースターショー	iisutaashoo
eat	食べます	tabemasu
eight	八	hachi
eighth day of the month	八日	yōka
elder brother	おにいさん；あに	
elder sister	おねえさん；あね	
email	eメール	iimeeru
English	えい語	eigo
English conversation	えいかいわ	
enjoyable	たのしい	
enter	はいります	
entrance	いりぐち	
entrance ceremony (school)	にゅう学しき	nyuugakushiki
ethics	どうとく	
event	イベント	ibento
every day	まい日	mainichi
every year	まい年	maitoshi
everyone	みなさん；みんな	
everyone together	みんなで	
exam	しけん	
excursion	えんそく	
excuse me	すみません	
exists	います (living things)；あります (non-living things)	
experiment	じっけん	
explain	せつめいする	
extra curricular activities	ならいごと	
eye	目	me

F

face	かお	
fairy floss	わたあめ	
family	かぞく	
famous	ゆうめい（な）	
fan	ファン	fan
fast	はやく	
father	お父さん　otōsan；父　chichi	
favourite	一ばん好き（な）　ichibansuki (na)；好き（な）　suki (na)	
February	二月	nigatsu
fencing (Japanese); kendo	けんどう	
festival	（お）まつり	
fine	はれ	
firefly	ほたる	
fireworks	はなび	
first day of the month	一日	tsuitachi
fishing	つり	
fit	げんき（な）	
food	食べもの	
foot	あし	
football	フットボール	futto booru
forum	フォーラム	fōramu

fourth day of the month	四日	yokka
free (such as time)	ひま（な）	
Friday	金よう日	kinyōbi
fried noodles	やきそば	
friend	ともだち	
from	から	
fruit	くだもの	
full	（おなかが）いっぱい	
full stop	まる	
fun	たのしい	
funny	おもしろい	
furthermore	それに	

G

game	ゲーム	geemu
game; match	しあい	
garden	にわ	
generally	たいてい	
gentle	やさしい	
geography	ちり	
get up	おきます	
gift	プレゼント	purezento
gift card	ギフトカード	gifutokaado
Gion festival	ぎおん まつり	
girl; girls	女の子	onnanoko
go	行きます	ikimasu
go home	かえります	
go in	はいります	
good	いい；よい	
good (was)	よかった	
good at	とくい（な）	
goodbye	バイバイ	baibai (casual)
good-looking	かっこいい	
good morning	おはよう (casual); おはよう ございます (polite)	
goods	グッズ	guzzu
gorgeous	すてき（な）	
grammar	ぶんぽう	
grandfather	おじいさん；そ父	sofu
grandmother	おばあさん；そ母	sobo
great	すごい	
green tea	（お）ちゃ	
group	グループ	guruupu
guitar	ギター	gitaa
gymnastics	たいそう	

H

hair	かみ（のけ）	
half	半	han
hand	手	te
hang in there!	がんばれ！	
hang out	あそびます	
happi coat	はっぴ	
happy	うれしい	
happy birthday	（お）たんじょう日 おめでとう (o) tanjōbi omedetō (casual); おたんじょう日 おめでとう ございます o tanjōbi omedeto gozaimasu (polite)	
Harajuku (city in Tokyo)	原宿	harajuku
hard; difficult	むずかしい	
hat	ぼうし	
have (*a shower*)	あびます	
head	あたま	
healthy	げんき（な）	
height (body height)	せ	
here	ここ；こちら	
here you are	どうぞ	
heart beating sound	ドキドキ	dokidoki
hey	ねえこら	
history	れきし	

hobby	しゅみ	
holiday	休み	yasumi
home	うち	
home economics	かていか	
homeroom	ホームルーム	hōmuruumu
homework	しゅくだい	
hoodie	パーカー	paakaa
host family	ホスト ファミリー	hosuto famirii
hotdog	ホットドッグ	hotto doggu
hour	時かん	jikan
house	うち	
how	何で	nande
how many people	何人	nannin
how old	何さい	nansai
how was it?	どう でしたか	
hundred	百	
100-yen shop	100円ショップ	hyaku en shoppu

I

I	わたし；ぼく (for a boy)	
ice skating	アイス スケート	aisu sukeeto
Iga	伊賀	iga
important	たいせつ（な）	
indoor shoes	うわばき	
interesting	おもしろい	
interview	インタビュー	intabyuu
is	います (living things); あります (non-living things)	
is; am	です	
is; am	でございます (polite)	
is not (living things)	いません	
is not ——	～じゃない です	
isn't it?	ですね	

J

jacket	ジャケット	jaketto
January	一月	ichigatsu
Japan	日本	nihon
Japanese animation	ジャパニメ	japanime
Japanese language	日本語	nihongo
Japanese language; national language	こく語	kokugo
Japanese person	日本人	nihonjin
Japanese-style	わふう	
Jazz	ジャズ	jazu
jeans	ジーンズ	jiinzu
J-pop	Jポップ	jee poppu
judo	じゅうどう	
July	七月	shichigatsu
jumper	セーター	seetaa
June	六月	rokugatsu
junior high school	中学校	chuugakkō
junior high school student	中学生	chuugakusei

K

karaoke	カラオケ	karaoke
karate	からて	
keep well	げんきでね！	
kendo; Japanese fencing	けんどう	
kind	やさしい	
Kumamoto prefecture	熊本県	kumamoto ken

L

last week	先しゅう	
last year	きょ年	kyonen
learn	ならいます	
left	ひだり	
leg	あし	
lesson	レッスン	ressun

Vocabulary

like	好き（な） suki (na); 好き です suki desu
line	ぎょう
listen	ききます
little bit	ちょっと
live	すんでいます
lively	にぎやかな
lollies	（お）かし
long	ながい
look	見ます mimasu
look!	見て！ mite
lots	たくさん
love; really like	大好き（な） daisuki (na)
lunch	（お）ひるごはん
lunch box	（お）べんとう
lunch break	ひる休み hiruyasumi

M

magazine	ざっし
make	つくります
man; men	男の人 otokonohito
manga	まんが
manga café	まんがきっさ
many	たくさん
March	三月 sangatsu
mascot	マスコット masukotto
mask	おめん
Master	～ちゃん chan
match	しあい
mathematics	すう学 suugaku
May	五月 gogatsu
may I have [item]?	～を ください
may I interrupt you?	ちょっと いい ですか
me	わたし；ぼく (for a boy)
meat	にく
meet	あいます
member	メンバー menbaa
merchandise	グッズ guzzu
milk	ぎゅうにゅう
minute	分 fun; pun; bun
Miss	～ちゃん
mobile phone	けいたい でんわ；ケータイ keetai (slang)
Monday	月よう日 getsuyōbi
moon	月 tsuki
more	もっと
morning	あさ
mother	お母さま okaasama (polite); お母さん okaasan
mountain	山 yama
mouth	口 kuchi
movie	えいが
Mr (for young men and boys)	～くん
mum	お母ちゃん okaachan; 母 haha
music	おんがく
musical	ミュージカル myuujikaru
my	わたしの；ぼくの (for a boy)
myself	わたし；ぼく (for a boy)

N

national language; Japanese	こく語 kokugo
Nara	奈良 nara
navigator service	ナビサービス nabisaabisu
neck tie	ネクタイ nekutai
netball	ネットボール netto booru
never	ぜんぜん ～ません
new	あたらしい
next	つぎ
nice; gentle	やさしい
nice; gorgeous	すてき（な）
nice to see/meet you	どうぞ よろしく おねがい します (polite); どうぞ よろしく (casual)
night	よる
ninja	にんじゃ
ninja house	にんじゃしき
no	いいえ
nose	はな
not at all	ぜんぜん ～ません
not much	あまり；あんまり
not often	あまり ～ません；あんまり ～ません
not yet	まだ
November	十一月 juuichigatsu
now	いま

O

ocean	うみ
o'clock	～時 ji
October	十月 juugatsu
octopus dumplings	たこやき
often	よく
oh	ああ
OK	オッケー okkee
old	ふるい
on foot	あるいて
one	一 ichi
one hundred	百 hyaku
one more time; once again	もう いちど
one person	一人 hitori
online game	オンラインゲーム onrain geemu
only child	一人っこ hitorikko
origami	おりがみ
Osaka castle	大阪じょう ōsaka jō
other	ほか

P

packed lunch	（お）べんとう
pancake with sweet red bean	どらやき
pants	パンツ pantsu
(my) parents	りょうしん
paragraph	だんらく
park	こうえん
party	パーティー paatii
PE	たいいく
Peace Park	へいわこうえん
perform	えんそうします
period ——	～時かんめ jikanme
period one	１時かんめ ichijikanme
person	人 hito
photo	しゃしん
physical education	たいいく
piano	ピアノ piano
pickles	つけもの
picture	え
picture diary	えにっき
place	ところ
play (a musical instrument)	ひきます
play (a sport)	します
play; have fun	あそびます
play; perform	えんそう します
please	ください
please do your best	がんばって ください
pocket money	（お）こづかい
pool	プール puuru
poor thing	かわいそう
popular	にんきが あります；にんきが ある
portable shrine	ほこ
poster	ポスター posutaa
potato	じゃがいも
pottery	やきもの yakimono
practice	れんしゅう
precious	たいせつ（な）

百十四

114

present	プレゼント	purezento
pretty	きれい（な）	
primary school	小学校	shōgakkō
primary school student	小学生	shōgakusei
profile	プロフィール	purofiiru
put on (shoes)	はきます	

Q

questionnaire	アンケート	ankeeto
quickly	はやく	
quiet	しずか（な）	

R

rare	めずらしい	
rarely	あまり　〜ません；あんまり　〜ません	
read	よみます	
reading (as a hobby)	どくしょ	
really	ほんとう；ほんとうに	
receive	もらいます	
restaurant	レストラン	resutoran
return	かえります	
rice	ごはん；ライス	
rice ball	おにぎり	
ride	のります	
right	みぎ	
river	川	kawa
robot	ロボット	robotto
rock 'n' roll	ロック	rokku
room	へや	

S

saffron rice	サフランライス	safuran raisu
samurai	さむらい	
sandals	サンダル	sandaru
Saturday	土よう日	doyōbi
say	いいます	
scarf	マフラー	mafuraa
scary	こわい	
school	学校	gakkō
school bus	スクールバス	sukuurubasu
school culture festival	ぶんかさい	
school grounds	グラウンド	guraundo
school lunch	きゅうしょく	
school subject	かもく	
school trip	しゅう学りょこう	shuugakuryoko
science	りか；か学	kagaku
scrapbook	スクラップブック	sukurappubukku
sea	うみ	
second day of the month	2日	futsuka
see	見ます	mimasu
see you (later)	じゃあ（ね）	
see you tomorrow	また　あした	
self-introduction	じこしょうかい	
sell	うります	
senior high school	高校	kōkō
senior high school student	高校生	kōkō sei
September	九月	kugatsu
service	サービス	saabisu
seventh day of the month	七日	nanoka
shinkansen	しんかんせん	
shop	みせ	
shopping	買いもの	kaimono
short	みじかい	
short (height)	（せが）ひくい	
show bag	ショーバッグ	shoobaggu
shower	シャワー	shawaa
shrine	じんじゃ	

siblings	きょうだい	
similar	にている	
sing	うたいます	
sister (elder)	おねえさん；あね	
sister (younger)	いもうとさん；いもうと	
six	六	roku
sixth day of the month	六日	muika
ski	スキー	skii
skillfully	じょうずに	
skirt	スカート	sukaato
sleep	ねます	
slippers	うわばき	
slowly	ゆっくり	
small	小さい	chiisai
sneakers	スニーカー	suniikaa
soccer	サッカー	sakkaa
socks	ソックス	sokkusu
social sciences	しゃかい	
sometimes	ときどき	
sounds good	いいですね	
song	うた	
Sony	ソニー	sonii
soup	スープ	suupu
souvenir	（お）みやげ	
surprised	おどろいた	
sports	スポーツ	supōtsu
sports clubs	うんどうぶ	
sports festival	たいいくさい	
spring	はる	
stall	やたい	
stamp (postage)	きって	
station	えき	
stay	とまります	
stay at home	うちにいます	haruyasumi
spring holiday	はる休み	
spring roll	はるまき	
stomach	おなか	
strange	へん（な）	
strict	きびしい	
stroll	さんぽ	
strong	つよい	
strong at	とくい（な）	
student	学生	gakusei
study	べんきょう　します	
subject	かもく	
sukiyaki (a Japanese meal)	すきやき	
summer	なつ	
summer holiday	なつ休み	natsuyasumi
sun	日	hi
Sunday	日よう日	nichiyōbi
sunny	はれ	
sweets	（お）かし	
swimming	すいえい	
swimming carnival	すいえいたいかい	
sword	かたな	

T

tail	しっぽ	
take	とります	
take (a shower)	あびます	
take care	きを　つけてね	
talk	はなします	
tall (height)	（せが）高い	(se ga) takai
Tanabata festival	たなばたまつり	
taxi	タクシー	takushii
teacher	先生	
technology	ぎじつ	
television	テレビ	terebi
temple	（お）てら	
tennis	テニス	tenisu

115

百十五

Vocabulary

English	Japanese	Romaji
tent	テント	tento
tenth day of the month	十日	tōka
Term One	一学き	ichigakki
Term Three	三学き	sangakki
Term Two	二学き	nigakki
terrible	いやだ	
test	テスト	tesuto
thanks (*an expression of*) said before eating	いただきます	
thank you	ありがとう (*casual*); ありがとう ございました (*polite*) サンキュー	sankyuu
theatre	えんげき	
then	じゃ；では	
therefore	だから	
third day of the month	三日	mikka
this person	この人	hito
this place	ここ	
this time	こんど	
throwing star	しゅりけん	
Thursday	木よう日	mokuyōbi
time	時かん *jikan*；時	toki
timetable	時かんわり	jikanwari
toast	トースト	tōsuto
today	きょう	
together	いっしょに	
tomorrow	あした	
too	も	
town	まち	
Toyota	トヨタ	toyota
train	でんしゃ	
true	ほんとう	
t-shirt	T-シャツ	tii shatsu
Tuesday	火よう日	kayōbi
twentieth day of the month	二十日	hatsuka
twenty years old	はたち	
twinkle twinkel	キラキラ	kirakira
two	二	ni
two people	二人	futari

U

umm	ちょっと	
understood	わかりました	
understand	わかります	
uniform	せいふく	
Uniqlo	ユニクロ	yunikuro
university	大学	daigaku
until	まで	
unusual	めずらしい	
use	つかいます	
usually	たいてい	

V

various	いろいろ（な）	
very	とても	
vest	ベスト	besuto

W

wake up	おきます	
walk	さんぽ；あるきます	
walking	あるいて	
was	でした	
watch	見ます	mimasu
watch; clock	とけい	
water	水	mizu
we	ぼくたち (*for boys*); わたしたち (*for girls*)	
weak at	にがて（な）	
wear	きます (*clothes*)；はきます (*shoes*)；かぶります (*for head*)	
Wednesday	水よう日	suiyōbi
weekend	しゅうまつ	
welcome (*to a shop or restaurant*)	いらっしゃいませ	
well	じょうずに	
well done	よく できました	
well then	じゃ；じゃあ（ね）	
what	何	nan; nani
what day	何日	nannichi
what day (of the week)	何よう日	nanyōbi
what grade; what year level	何年生	nannensei
what kind of; what sort of	どんな	
what month	何月	nangatsu
what period	何時かんめ	nanjikanme
what should I do?	どうしよう	
what time	何時	nanji
when	いつ	
where	どこ	
which one of the three or more	どれ	
which one of the two (casual form)	どっち	
which person	どの人	donohito
who	だれ	
why	どうして；なぜ	
winter	ふゆ	
winter holiday	ふゆ休み	fuyuyasumi
with	と	
woman; women	女の人	onnanohito
woof woof (dog bark)	ワンワン	wan wan
word	ことば	
worldwide	せかい中	sekai juu
wow	わあ	
write	かきます	

Y

year	年	nen
Year level	～年生	nensei
—— years old	～さい	
yen	円	en
yes	はい	
yippee	やった	
younger brother	おとうとさん；おとうと	
younger sister	いもうとさん；いもうと	
yuck	いやだ	

Z

English	Japanese	Romaji
zero	ゼロ *zero*；れい	